FOUND AT LAST

A Journey of Family, Memory, and Belonging

MADLYN EPSTEIN STEINHART

Published: March 2026

Paperback ISBN: 979-8-9951103-0-9
Hardcover ISBN: 979-8-9947313-9-0
Library of Congress Control Number: 2026905532

For information address:
The Three Tomatoes Book Publishing
6 Soundview Rd.
Glen Cove, NY 11542

Cover design: Susan Herbst
Interior design: Susan Herbst

Disclaimer: This book chronicles the author's exploration of family roots using historical documents, public records, and personal accounts. All information is presented to the best of the author's knowledge. Genealogical research can contain gaps, inconsistencies, or evolving interpretations; therefore, this book should be viewed as a personal narrative rather than an authoritative genealogical source. Any references to individuals outside the author's documented lineage are unintentional.

DEDICATION

*In memory of my parents, grandparents,
great-grandparents, aunts, uncles, and cousins.*

Searching

*It is one thing to grow up with incomplete information
about your family.*

*Whoever had the answers chose not to elaborate
or fill in the blanks.*

*It was a different time and place where questions
were not asked because you would not get an answer,
and asking questions would get you into trouble.*

*The answers, even at this point, are incomplete,
and we have to leave things as they are.*

*Stop guessing about the origins and move forward
with relationships that are still blossoming into a family.*

What defines family and how it works is a continuing story.

PREFACE

Family is defined as all descendants of a common ancestor. What happens when you don't have a complete family story? Genealogy is creating a story of family history. Menachem (Manya) Meeninyeetza Mandel is our great-grandfather. Yetta Perlmutter (Perelmuth) is our great-grandmother.

Have you ever felt incomplete, as if something deep inside was somehow missing? Do the idyllic celebrations and milestones in your life somehow make you long for something more complete? Have you ever had the feeling that you know there has to be more? I admit that's what happened to me.

Let me tell you a little about myself. I'm a middle-aged woman who is shy and very sensitive. I love to cook, read, play slot machines, and travel, especially to Toronto and London. I love to write free-style poetry. Writing is my form of therapy, healing, and relaxation. It's my personal freedom... sort of a security blanket with words. I like comedy and humor, but I'm not thrilled with sarcasm. It can hurt.

I could get lost in an art or history museum for hours, then come back the next day and visit all over again. I love Chinese food, BBQ, and salads. Offer me fish, and I'll be your new best friend. My tastes in music range from Neil Diamond to Michael Bublé to Lady Gaga. We won't even discuss my love for teddy bears and Snoopy. I take a daily exercise walk, or two, where I play with many of the dogs in the neighborhood. Believe me, I'm physically and emotionally grateful for these walks. Growing up, I had a few friends, all of whom went on to successful careers. Some of these friends I still see today.

I miss my parents very much and love them both, but almost five years ago, there was an awful lot of information about the paternal side of my family that I knew very little or nothing about. Why people in the family seldom visited us, or we didn't visit them, was not questioned because children were to be seen, not heard, in the sixties and seventies... or at least, that was how it was in my family. You accept that and move on with your life, but somehow, deep inside, you know something is missing... a sense of familial connection and history. The people in this book are all related to my great-grandfather.

I know I wasn't adopted. There's enough proof, so I can say that unequivocally. Family resemblances alone prove that, but not knowing my family, or even knowing of their existence, sometimes made me feel even worse than if I wasn't adopted. That's left for discussion on another day. Yes, there are emotional scars.

I helped a client as a search angel, a volunteer who assisted adopted people in finding information about their birth families. My rule was that once the research was completed, the clients were given the information, and then they could choose the next step.

My research skills as a search angel prepared me more than I realized. I spent hours in the Dorot Jewish Division of the New York Public Library. Many websites, including Ancestry.com, Genealogybank.com, Geni.com, YadVashem.com, JewishGen.org, and FamilySearch.org, proved to be helpful. Other excellent sources to help in genealogical research are FindMyPast.com and the National Genealogical Society, which can offer educational resources. I thank all of them.

When I finished my work, I wished the client well, then said, "Goodbye." However, there was a DNA match in my own life that kept haunting me. Several unsuccessful attempts to contact this mystery relative created more questions, but no response was forthcoming. Why didn't this person answer me? I was getting frustrated.

I knew I had to go beyond birth, death, and marriage certificates. Yes, these records can provide huge amounts of information, but to discover history, I needed more. Family members might have documents, but first, I had to find my family members.

I never had a "bucket list" of things I wanted to do, but finding my family jumped to the top of the list of what I had to do. I wouldn't say I was obsessed; however, I was more than consumed. Who were these people who were out there? I don't know if the need came from the want, or if the want came from the need. Either way, I had to do this. I could not live with myself if I didn't work on this project. I gave it another try.

I wasn't sure if I should take a leap of faith at this point and then pivot, but there was a closed door that needed to be opened… and I wanted to open it quickly. The more I thought about it, I knew I had to act. Finding a relative, any relative, would make me happy. I knew my maternal cousins. Who and where were my paternal ones?

I have theories about why my parents didn't tell us about relatives I later discovered—theories that I wish I could prove. I had to throw those theories to the wind because the answers and people are gone. Unfortunately, heaven doesn't have visiting hours. My father never talked about his family. Why? Was he trying to protect us? What or who was he trying to protect us from? Why keep this information a secret? Did my family have ghosts in the closet? What may have happened? My immediate family comes from an educated family that has achieved. We should have been told that.

The main theory is that some of my grandmother's siblings did not get along, so we did not know them, nor they, us. What used to be no longer counts. My cousins have suspicions, but they, too, don't know why. We have questions. We don't have logical answers. It's sad to be excluded from your family history, which is exactly what happened to my sister, cousins, and me.

Was no family contact intentional? Did someone do something to create this family schism? Was there some objective at the time that no one spoke of? Who started all of this? Lots of questions with no answers.

How does a family fall apart? How does a family not keep in touch? Was there a family feud? What happened to my family? One might be thinking, why should it matter, and matter now? It matters because it is a connection to my late father and information my family needs to share and pass down to younger generations. We want to know our family history. Closure would be wonderful.

My newly discovered paternal family lives in Oklahoma, California, Massachusetts, Texas, New York, Florida, and Italy. Distance is not a problem among the new cousins, but we wonder why our parents didn't reach out since they were all first cousins. Two of those elderly cousins are still living but have not shared much information with us. They know more but are not telling what they know. Several of the younger cousins, including me, have asked repeatedly, but we have no answers from our elders.

My paternal grandmother never said much about members of her family. She had seven brothers and sisters. I met two of her sisters when I was little and two of her brothers when my father died in 1973, but there was not much conversation given the circumstances.

My conclusion is that somewhere along the way, for whatever reason, people didn't talk or had a disagreement; therefore, there was little to no communication at all. I can only imagine the "family drama" that took place. You can't treat an open wound with a Band-Aid.

There was a visit to Florida in 1974, but I remember only names, not faces. We met my father's first cousin, Sydell, along with Uncle Jack and his wife, Anna. To my knowledge, no one has given any information about our relatives and family history. It wasn't discussed... at least not around my sister and me.

Please don't misunderstand, there are no pointing fingers or blaming of people. In a family of eight siblings, bad blood is bound to happen. Not knowing who people are, especially in your own family, is a mystery for the ages. I didn't want to accept that. I haven't.

I am incredibly happy to say that I have reconnected with my second cousins and am still learning about them, their parents, and their families... real genetic cousins whom I love dearly that have become part of my family.

The greatest lesson learned from the last five years is that everybody, whether they are adopted or not, should know their families. I always felt that there was nothing special about my family... but I was wrong! Every family is and was special. Sometimes you just have to look a little harder and dig a little deeper to find the gems.

This is the story of how I found the paternal side of my family and how learning about them and our family history, or "herstory," has made me feel more authentic. This book is dedicated in memory of my parents, grandparents, great-grandparents, aunts, uncles, and cousins.

TABLE OF CONTENTS

Chapter 1

DISCOVERING FAMILY

ROWING UP, I FELT THAT people were missing from my life. My paternal grandfather died over twenty years before I was born. My father barely spoke to us about him, other than to say he fed squirrels in the park by placing peanuts in his pockets. The squirrels would take the nuts right out of his pockets. For years, I didn't even know what he did for a living. My maternal grandparents and my maternal great-aunt and great-uncle were among the few who visited us.

My father, Manuel (Manny) Epstein, was born in Brooklyn, New York, on March 9, 1928. He passed away in our apartment on August 23, 1973. He was a loner, and I believe that I inherited that personality trait from him. My mother and sister were, and are, more family-oriented than I. We were all devastated when he passed. I internalized so much grief for so many years. My interest in genealogy helped heal deep wounds and pain. I can thank my mother-in-law, Bonnie, for helping develop my interest in genealogy.

Looking for the paternal side of my family while assisting clients as a search angel did not seem to fit who I was. I'm the quiet, unassuming one. Reaching out to others just wasn't me. It's a good thing I enjoy research, because there was a lot of work to be done to uncover what I didn't know. There are always more questions to be answered. Each answered question led to another unopened door—not easy for a sensitive, shy person.

It seemed my social skills improved as an adult, even though I tend to be more of a loner than my family recognizes. I was about to unlock my stories, but the greatest one was about the disconnection within the family. "Heaven Only Knows" became my mantra.

My new nickname is "The Family Detective," because when one page ends, you turn the page and more information comes up. Those words would soon be prophetic. It was long overdue to get answers. There was so much I didn't know about my ancestors.

I started with what I knew. My great-grandparents, Menachem and Yetta, had eight children: Mary, Bella, Gussie, Tillie, Bertha, Anna, Paul, and Jack. Some of those faceless names were about to come alive. I was about to explore a new world about my own family—a world that hadn't spoken to me before. Diving into the past, I felt as if I were the CEO of a new company, and my distant relatives were my shareholders. It's nice to have everyone reporting to me.

The Main Branch of the New York Public Library at

Fifth Avenue and 42nd Street in Manhattan became my home away from home. The gorgeous Beaux-Arts building, with its famed lions, Patience and Fortitude, guarding the Fifth Avenue entrance, has first-floor and third-floor research rooms where I took up weekly, if not daily, residence. Armed with pads of legal-sized note paper and a special pen my husband gave me, I sat in the blissful quiet of the research rooms, searching through website after website looking for any record of people I had never known.

On days I didn't go to the library, I made a couple of trips to the New York City Search Center, which is within the West End Collegiate Church at 241 West 77th Street in Manhattan. The Church and Search Center are run by the Mormons, who are strong advocates of genealogical research. Workers there were very helpful and wished me luck in my search. Through this agency, I volunteered as a virtual search angel, assisting adoptees searching for their families.

Another place I visited was The Center for Jewish History, located at 15 West 16th Street, also in Manhattan. They were incredibly helpful in finding cemeteries and cemetery maps. This is where I found my paternal grandfather, Milton Epstein, and my paternal great-grandfather, William Epstein. The Mandel Family research was started here. This organization strongly suggested that I research Mt. Hebron Cemetery in Queens for more information.

The archives and library in the Manhattan Municipal Building, now known as the David N. Dinkins Municipal Building at 1 Centre Street, is where I found out that

Meeninyeetza became Milciner, which later became Mandel. A representative there helped find the different names. This was before I even knew about the name Meeninyeetza.

I had already done a DNA swab test on Ancestry.com. Little did I expect that the results of the DNA test would alter the course of my life. Science doesn't lie, and the DNA facts awakened me to a new family that I didn't know about and now had to search for. On the website, there was a list of people with whom I shared DNA. I recognized a few names but had no clue about others. Who were they? How were they connected to me? Through Ancestry.com, I sent out numerous emails.

I met my cousin, Alex Resnick, through a DNA match on Ancestry.com. He finally answered my emails. Alex's DNA match had a centimorgan (cM) measurement of over 330, so I knew this person had to be a cousin, but how? Centimorgan measurement is a scientific term used to determine how closely one person is genetically related to another based on a swab test. The higher the cM reading, the closer the second person is to you.

Alex said he would call his cousin, Alex Chester, in Florida, who might know more about the family. Alex R. asked me for contact information, which I gladly shared. It took six minutes until my phone rang.

The voice said, "Hi, I am your cousin, Alex Chester, and I think our grandmothers were sisters. Was her maiden name Mandel?" I knew that was my paternal grandmother's last name. I screamed out, "Yes!" Alex said again,

"Our grandmothers were sisters!" I now had two new cousins, both named Alex... Alex R. and Alex C.

The person who was the DNA match on Ancestry, Alex Resnick, shared the same grandmother as the person who called me, Alex Chester. Gussie, who later changed her name to Jean, was their grandmother... my great-aunt. Our parents were first cousins. The two Alexes and I are second cousins.

Would my "new" cousins help me? Both Alexes stayed in touch. We shared information, but there was so much more to learn. This is the beginning of how I found the paternal side of my family. Curiosity began to take over our thoughts. Who or what would we find next?

Alex R. mentioned that he knew that some family lived in Florida. During the conversation, my Uncle Paul was mentioned. Alex R. reminded me that Paul was his grandmother Gussie's brother, as well as my grandmother Bertha's brother. Alex R. went on to say that he thought Uncle Paul's granddaughter lived in Florida and her name was Rona.

A few days later, I located Rona on social media. I sent her a message asking if her mother's name was Sydell? The reply was instantaneous. Rona said, "Yes! I knew family was out there!" Rona also told me that she had a sister named Dona.

Rona's mother, Sydell, was close to my father, Manny. Rona told me that her sister, Dona, remembered their mother mentioning the name Manny. I knew my father had a cousin in Florida whom he was close to named

Sydell. Ding! Ding! Ding! Why didn't our father tell us about Rona and Dona? Unanswered question.

My DNA matches to Rona, Dona, and Alex R. are 382cM, 376cM, and 335cM. These are significant numbers. Rona, Dona, and the two Alexes have become part of the family that I never knew I had. Meeting them was a gift I could never have imagined. They helped make me whole. My list of "new" cousins had just doubled! I was just getting started.

I now had a team of cousins who were just as curious as I was about finding out more about our family and what may have happened decades ago. We immediately shared what we knew off the top of our heads and set out looking for more. Long-distance telephone calls suddenly became part of a weekly routine. Monthly weekend Zoom meetings allowed us to stay in touch and share what we were able to learn. Soon, the Zoom meetings expanded from four or five new cousins to double digits as more relatives wanted to be involved. More new cousins were now part of my life! My family was growing beyond what I had ever dreamed of. With each phone call or Zoom meeting, there was so much excitement pulsing through my body. For some reason, I found myself talking louder than I normally did. My family noticed that, too!

After lots of research into my family and building a new, larger family tree, my new cousins and I reveled in our discoveries. The more my family and I connected, the greater the eagerness to learn more. We all searched for documents and shared stories about what and who we found.

We frequently logged in to Ancestry.com so we could update our family trees. Finding a document on a website was a delicious treat, subsequently shared by many.

With each new piece of information received, I felt as if my ancestors were speaking to me. All of a sudden, it seemed as if they knew me and were talking directly to me, asking me, "Where have you been? We have a lot to discuss!" I reached out to them. Now they were reaching back.

In January 2020, good fortune smiled upon my family when we found out that many relatives who either didn't know each other or hadn't seen each other in many years (in some cases, decades) were all going to be in Florida at the same time. "The Family Detective" set out to plan a party so everyone could meet. I had no idea what I was getting into, but something was telling me I had to do this. I planned to focus attention on the cousins, not me. It was left to me to connect the dots of a family I was part of but still learning about.

What better place to have a Jewish family reunion than in a Kosher deli? I contacted the event planner at Ben's Kosher Deli in Boca Raton. We planned for seventeen people with a menu of appetizers, pastrami and corned beef sandwiches, side dishes, and a decorated layer cake for dessert. Of course, there would be plenty of Dr. Brown's sodas. What else goes with a deli sandwich? The party was on! Now we had to tell everyone to show up!

Phone calls, text messages, and emails were sent out. Almost immediately, cousins from Oklahoma, Alex R. and his wife, Jane, said they'd be there early to help. Alexa and Marvin from Massachusetts couldn't wait for the date. My Florida cousins were all in. Rona and Dona wanted to help in any way they could. Now the countdown to the date began. Three weeks to the party.

Unfortunately, the California cousins and upstate New York cousins could not attend. We planned a family Zoom meeting for after the party so the missing relatives could be a part of the festivities. We weren't leaving out anyone whom we could find.

Finally, the big day arrived. Cousins driving north, south, and east to, at long last, see and meet each other in Boca. Where was Route 441? Has anybody heard of Clint Moore Rd.? How fast could I get there? A few speed limits were broken. Curiosity? Anticipation? The song *Mr. Big Stuff* by Jean Knight, with the lyric *Who Do You Think You Are?* kept running through my mind. I arrived early. My life hasn't been the same since. I wanted to immediately reach out to all of my discoveries. Was the introvert becoming an extrovert? Regarding this subject, I think the answer was "Yes!"

When the partyers arrived, I met Lois and Marty, Alex R. and Jane, Alex C. and Sherry, Marv and Alexa, and a few more, all for the first time. Alex C. and Lois are brother and sister. The reason for all the "A" names is that they were named after their grandfather, Alexander, my great-uncle.

Hugging, handshakes, kisses, and tears started immediately. Pointing at faces, looking at resemblances, and remembering long-lost relatives was a major occurrence throughout the party. A wall adorned with photos backed up what we saw. It was hard to believe that so many of these people were related to my father. I felt as if I was reaching into the past, and the past was reaching back out to me.

Howard, the restaurant waiter, wanted to start serving food, but with so much conversation going on, we delayed the meal. Everyone wanted to meet new cousins or reunite with old ones. About an hour into the event, food was served.

The party lasted about three and a half hours, but the time flew by too quickly. We needed more time. Immediately, I thought of a second reunion but wanted someone else to plan it. I gave out blank family trees as party favor souvenirs so people could fill in their own trees. *Photographs and Memories* may be a Jim Croce song, but it was a perfect theme for the party. I kept thinking that our great-grandparents, grandparents, and parents were all smiling down at us from heaven. My family was back! Who thought that one small party would affect people's lives for years?

Phone calls and the Zoom meeting after the party lasted until late at night. Everyone wanted more. Even the spouses of the cousins wanted to stay in touch. Some, including my husband, had relatives with similar last names on their family trees. More research to be done. People who knew nothing about each other, or had nothing in common, suddenly became connected because of new, previously unconnected genealogical research. Strangers became friends and family. The seeds were planted for annual visits and shared meals, and yes, we've carried through on this promise. My family dynamics were changed forever!

If a family is built on a solid foundation, I—and we—have been blessed to have a sturdy one.

Chapter 2

RONA OPENS A DOOR

FINDING MY COUSIN RONA WAS a tremendous help in organizing a confusing jigsaw puzzle. Not only did she help identify border pieces, but she was able to fill in the vast puzzle center. Rona and I talked for hours, with her filling me in about Uncle Paul and Uncle Jack. Rona reinforced everything I knew and elaborated on the Mandel Family. I couldn't wait to get more information.

When my father, Manny, died in 1973 at age forty-five from a massive coronary, Rona's grandfather, Paul, and his brother, Jack (my great-uncles), flew to New York to visit their sister, Bertha, my dad's mom. The family was sitting Shiva (the Jewish tradition of mourning the dead) at our apartment in Sheepshead Bay. Family and friends came to pay their respects and comfort those of us who were grieving. Many of them brought food, so we didn't have to cook.

I remembered Paul and Jack taking my Grandmother Bertha home to her tiny apartment in the Midwood section of Brooklyn. I had never seen Paul or Jack before this, but I knew that Paul's daughter was Sydell, my dad's first cousin. My family was growing at a tragic time of loss.

In 1974, my mother, sister, and I visited South Florida. It was our first trip since our dad passed away. I had never been on a plane before, and it was fun. Ft. Lauderdale was hot! Cousin Sydell picked us up at the airport and took us to Uncle Jack and Aunt Anna's house. Uncle Paul and his wife, Aunt Betty, were not there. I wondered why.

To this day, I remember the names, but barely the faces. I know there was a lot of conversation happening that I was not part of—adults-only conversation. It didn't bother me. The shy loner hardly said anything. I was happier in our hotel room after the get-together.

When my dad passed away, Rona and her sister, Dona, lived on Long Island. They knew nothing about my dad, nor his death, but their parents and grandparents had to know. This haunts me to this day because Uncle Paul's daughter, Sydell, was close to our father, her first cousin. No one said anything years ago, and no one in Rona and Dona's family knows today. Rona's father, the late Martin Kalb, remembered my dad but didn't know why there was a disconnect. When I met and talked to him, he definitely remembered my dad and wondered what had happened, the same as his daughters did. Perhaps this could all be chalked up to family politics. All we could do was speculate as to what led to what was. We had no answers to pressing family questions.

Even though Rona and I talked on the phone so many times, meeting her and her husband, Mike, was something special. We met at a new restaurant, Havana 1957 Cuban Cuisine, located in a tony, upscale outdoor shopping mall in Pembroke Pines, Florida. Rona, Mike, my husband, Howie, and I chatted for hours. It was a special night. In all honesty, I was so engrossed in the conversation and pages of notes I took that I don't even remember what we ate! FYI... I like Cuban food.

Rona and I also shared another commonality that we explored that night. We were both retired educators—Rona, a former kindergarten teacher, and I, a middle and high school teacher. Needless to say, we shared our war stories, talking about our mutual love of being in the class-room and how and why we both got into education. It's always nice to talk about the success stories we've had.

Rona is always asking me about what I've discov-ered. She is always at the ready to share what she knows while encouraging me to find out more. Now that she was really interested in genealogy, I helped her get started with her own Ancestry.com account. This search angel is now teaching other family members how to do genealogical research. Professor Henry Louis Gates would be proud of me! And I'm very proud of Rona for starting and continu-ing her genealogical research.

I told Rona that the process of genealogical research could be very emotionally draining. She would experience the highs of discovery combined with the lows and frus-trations of failure and inaccuracies. She had to "Keep on truckin'."

Rona's search into her family tree has already proven

fruitful. Through her father, she is related to former CBS News reporters Marvin and the late Bernard Kalb, both esteemed journalists with distinguished careers.

Rona and Dona not only have accepted me with loving, open arms as their "baby cousin," but have treated me as a sister. We meet a few times a year during my annual trips to Florida. While I chat with Rona, our husbands pass the time watching and discussing sports, memorabilia, and trading cards. The boys have their interests; we have ours.

Within minutes on each occasion, the family comes up. They cannot wait until we share family dinners, where the research results and family stories flow. I love seeing them! My cousins are much more outgoing than I am. They love to be involved in large groups or group activities, while I prefer smaller ones. I'm quite content with a one-on-one experience. My cousins are trying to get me to be more like them.

While the two sisters are very close (even living next door to each other), Rona and Dona have distinct personalities. Rona is a proud Democrat, while Dona is a strong Republican. We've all agreed not to bring up politics at the lunch or dinner table. Our time together is too short to argue. Both are dedicated, loving mothers who excelled in raising their families. They'll both give you the shirts off their backs, looking to help whenever they can.

Shortly after I met Rona in person in 2020, she introduced me to her uncle, Martin Mandel, my Uncle Paul's son, my father's first cousin. I met Martin at Rona's father's birthday party. When I first met Martin, I had a puzzled look on my face. Martin could easily pass for the older gentleman in the Cambridge Paving Stone television commercials. They look so much alike that they could be twins. They're not, but the resemblance is amazing.

A few days later, following a family lunch at a Ft. Lauderdale restaurant, Martin invited the family back to his nearby, richly decorated waterfront condo, where he had a surprise for me.

When we arrived at Martin's condo, he began by showing off his extensive art collection of paintings and sculptures. Martin certainly found his niche in art appreciation! After talking about his collection, Martin came through with his surprise... photo albums that he wanted me to look through. One of the albums contained a photo of my dad as a nineteen-year-old at Martin's Bar Mitzvah in 1947.

I was shocked, to say the least! I had never seen a picture of my dad when he was that young! Martin and my dad knew each other, but my family and I knew nothing about this picture. It seemed as if I was looking at a visual time machine, taking me back over seventy years.

My paternal grandparents, Bertha and Milton Epstein, were in the same photo. I was amazed! The picture is not of the highest quality, but I consider it one of my prized possessions. In the picture, my grandfather, Milton, looked like the actor Don Ameche. This was only the second photo I had seen of him. Sadly, he passed away on July 4, 1954, three years before I was born.

This photo of my dad and my grandparents, preserved

in a photo album held by a cousin I had just recently met, initiated more research. Martin wanted to learn about me and my family just as much as I wanted to learn about him and his. We talked many times on the phone. He was a wonderful source of information, recalling family stories and always encouraging me to continue my genealogical research.

With each tale, talking with Martin reminded me of the 1960s ABC-TV series, *The Time Tunnel*, starring James Darren and Robert Colbert. Martin told many stories, introducing me to new family members and their experiences. A man I met in 2020 gave me the keys to unlock more family doors.

Martin lived in New York, New Jersey, Illinois, Florida, and St. Thomas in the United States Virgin Islands. He had careers in architecture and hairdressing, owning salons in Cranford, New Jersey, and Palm Passage, part of the downtown shopping area in Charlotte Amalie, the capital of St. Thomas.

The Cranford salon was in the original town courthouse. The salon was downstairs. Martin lived upstairs. Martin Mandel lived a long and varied life, passing away on September 23, 2023, at eighty-seven years of age. Shortly before his death, I remember watching Martin on MSNBC talking about his vote on Election Day. He was out early in the morning to ensure he cast his ballot. I was very proud of him.

When Rona and I recently discussed our family and what may have led to the decades-long disconnect, she

said, "It doesn't matter now because we're all together...
and you're the reason why." Thanks, Rona! I've loved every minute of getting people back together.

MADLYN EPSTEIN STEINHART

Chapter 3

WHO ARE THE MANDELS AND THE EPSTEINS?

WHILE RESEARCHING THIS BOOK, I had difficulty finding accurate birth and death dates, along with cemetery records, due to surname changes and multiple records of people with the same name. That was about to change. Early in the research process, I learned never to put my money on the nose of one horse until I had additional proof. Several times, I found matching names of those I thought were long-lost relatives, only to find they were not the people I was looking for.

One search even led to perfectly matching names for grandparents and great-grandparents. None of these people were related to me. When things didn't work out, it made me want to search more. The "Family Detective" quickly became aware that genealogical websites contain errors. Not everything is accurate, but the joy of a discovery made me feel as if I were responding to the roar of a crowd—my crowd. Yes, I'm guilty of the occasional fist in the air when I found success. My crowd demanded that of me.

According to the latest statistics on Ancestry.com, I have over thirty-five thousand DNA matches, more than twenty-five thousand alone on my paternal side. I was shocked to learn that I have over eight thousand two hundred DNA matches on both sides of my family, with roots tracing back to Poland, Russia, Canada, Wales, and Scotland. There are no common ancestors listed on Ancestry going back ten generations, but DNA doesn't lie. There had to have been marriages decades and centuries ago between cousins who didn't know they were related.

I later came to find that this was a fairly common occurrence. Ancestry.com says the last names of Horing, Friedman, Hoffman, Horowitz, Kravetz, Morganstern, Weinstein, Adelson, Adler, and Alicea are the top ten most common names associated with paternal matches. The last names of Abramowitz, Adler, Aksamit, Call, Chisilev, Chriss, Cker, Dnac, Drucker, and Eoa are associated with both sides of my family. My family has no idea who any of these people are. I have sent several emails to people with these names, with no success in finding anyone significantly close to me or my immediate family.

Another research issue was finding appropriate records. European territory was constantly changing. Some siblings were born in Russia, while others were born in Stoberwa (Stebechve), Poland. It all depended upon who won a military battle on any given day. Reading this, a burning sense of injustice came to mind, reliving world history through documents, but that is another issue best left to historians, scholars, politicians, and diplomats.

Those who survived the incomparable horrors have told their tales of capture, oppression, torture, and rescue. Their scars, both physical and emotional, last a lifetime and continue to do so for some. We can only imagine the sacrifices our ancestors made to stay alive.

The original family surname was Meeninyeetza, but it was changed to Miliciner when the family came to the United States. Some spellings list Melnyeetza, Malneser, and Milciner as the family name. Multiple documents have different spellings for the same family. I expected that, especially if people came through Ellis Island. It is known that many names of people emigrating from Europe had their surnames changed by United States Immigration Officers when they arrived in this country. Even members of the same family have spelled the names differently.

The search was on—frustrating at times, but on. I could picture my ancestors arriving in the United States and seeing the Statue of Liberty. Their lives changed forever as they started their journeys to become Americans.

When my immigrant ancestors first saw the Statue of Liberty as they sailed into New York Harbor, I doubt that any of them had heard of Emma Lazarus' poem *"The New Colossus,"* written in 1883, with its famous words, "Give me your tired, your poor, your huddled masses yearning to be free." My ancestors and millions similar to them are the subjects of the poem. Whether it be Russia, Poland, Germany, or anywhere else in the world, the Statue of Liberty and the words of the poem inspire all who come to our shores.

Madlyn Epstein Steinhart

Our great-grandfather was Menachem (Manya) Meeninyeetza Mandel. He was born in a small town, L'vivska, also known as Jagielniga L'Viv, in Ukraine on October 4, around the year 1870. On Ancestry, one document lists his birth year as 1884. That has to be incorrect. He owned a ranch in Ukraine, but there are no records to prove it. So many official records from that time were destroyed or are simply missing. According to family lore, he worked seven days a week tending to his ranch, living a hard life off the land. He died at age thirty-nine, allegedly gored to death by a bull.

It's an interesting story, especially if true. Despite several attempts, I have yet to find Menachem's death certificate. I have contacted the Consulates of Ukraine, Russia, and Poland. All three Consulates never responded—another unanswered question. Looking back one generation, Menachem's parents were Bernard David Meeninyeetza and his wife, Ida Rachel, my great-great-grandmother. We could not find her maiden name or any additional information about her.

In Ashkenazi Jewish tradition, newborn children are named after deceased relatives. Quite often, that relative would be a grandparent or great-grandparent. My father, Manny, was named after his grandfather, Menachem. When I was born, my middle name, Beth, was chosen to remember Menachem's father, Bernard. It is believed that naming a child after a relative who has passed honors the memory of that relative and encourages the child to learn more about that part of his or her family. A Jewish person can have a Hebrew name and a Jewish name in addition to their recorded given name.

Menachem's wife, Yetta (Jenta) Perlmutter Mandel, was our great-grandmother. She was my grandmother Bertha's mother. Yetta was born in Ratna, Russia, in 1869 and came to live in the United States in 1922 with her children, Bertha, Paul, and Anna. They arrived in New York City on July 25 aboard the S.S. Mount Clinton, leaving Hamburg, Germany, on July 18.

When the family came to the United States, they arrived, as many families did, a few at a time, not as a complete family. The heartbreaking loss of the family patriarch, Menachem, at a young age, led to his widow and children emigrating to America. It took many years until most of the family was together again.

Finding Yetta turned out to be a long adventure. According to New York City death records, Yetta died on June 2, 1955, in Brooklyn, New York. At first, I was confused because multiple documents say Yetta Perlmutter died in 1952, but that couldn't be my Yetta because we have a picture showing she was alive in 1953. Then the trail led me to another Yetta Mandel, who passed in 1956, but some facts, including her age, didn't add up. Back to the computer for more research!

Where was Yetta? Where was she buried? What stumped my family and me for the longest time regarding Yetta's information is that no cemetery had a record of a Yetta Mandel with matching dates of birth and death. Even the New York City Department of Health was unable to retrieve the Death Certificate in their death records because, according to them, the records for that time period were not digitized. They said it would take months to try to find the original certificate. I'm still waiting. Further research led to more accurate information.

Finally, after another telephone call to Montefiore Cemetery in Springfield Gardens in Queens, New York, we found that Yetta Mankel (a simple clerical error in spelling) is recorded as buried there; however, her headstone does say Yetta Mandel (proper spelling). The dates match my great-great-grandmother. Years of searching finally came to an end! My thanks to Francine Chiarotti from Montefiore Cemetery for her persistence and assistance. You solved the family mystery! As did many of her generation, Yetta belonged to a Society. She was a member of the *Chev. Athereth Zkeinim Society*, as confirmed by the cemetery.

Going back a generation, I found Yetta's parents, Jacob Perlmutter and Sheila Shandie, both born in Belarus in 1839.

According to family stories, Yetta always wore black and spoke only Yiddish, which is not the same language as Hebrew. My introduction to her was a photo in my parents' January 1953 wedding album. The album pages were deteriorating, but the pictures inside were still in excellent condition. My cousin, Alex Chester, identified her from a scan of that photo. I was fascinated. Who was she? Alex told me that Yetta had a "unique personality" and was quite the character. "They used to call her Yetta the Yenta," Alex chuckled. If you know the word, no explanation is necessary.

I wanted to learn more about the lady in the black dress. I couldn't imagine asking my mother to identify the little old lady in the black velvet hat in the photo. I asked anyway. My mother said she didn't remember who the lady was. Strange, it was her wedding! I put on my researcher's hat and went to work. I have since given my parents' wedding album to my niece, Loni, who adored her grandmother.

Yetta gave birth to eight children: Mary (1893), Beila (1894), Gussie (Jean) (1898), Tillie (1899), Jack (1902), Bertha, our paternal grandmother (1906), Paul (1908), and Anna (1912). Seven of Yetta's children were born in Stebechve.

The only exception was Beila (Bella), born in Wolyn, Poland. Beila, who later became Bella Springer, never emigrated to the United States. She chose to stay in Poland. The family offered to bring her to the United States, but according to her siblings, she wanted to stay in Poland. Something about her needing dental work was the issue. Truth or lore?

Beila married a man named Josef Springer, and they had two daughters, Menucha (honoring Beila's father) and Chaya, who were born in 1942. Beila and her daughters were killed in the Holocaust in Wolyn, Poland, in 1945. Her husband, Josef, died in the concentration camps of Auschwitz, also in 1945 (See documents 1, 2, 3). Beila and Josef never saw each other again after separation by the Nazis. They never had the chance to escape their fate and follow their dreams.

My cousins did not know what happened to Beila. Most did not know she was married and had children until research proved otherwise. Many thanks to my cousin, Jake Garfinkle, for finding this and putting this information in his thesis.

Yetta's eldest daughter, Mary, married a man named William Mandel. When Mary and William married, the entire family, including Yetta and her husband Menachem, took that surname. Some family members later chose Mandell as the spelling of their name, adding an "L." Legal documents show both spellings. William was born on August 20, 1886, in Talmar, Russia. Mary and William married on June 8, 1914. William (recorded as Mandell) is listed as having passed away on March 21, 1955, at age sixty-eight. He was a member of the *Erste Zloczower Society* and is buried in Mt. Carmel Cemetery in Glendale, New York. Mary Mandel passed away on February 8, 1974, in Cleveland, Ohio. She was eighty years old.

Mary Mandel had three daughters: Minnie, Lillian, and Beatrice. Minnie Mandell (notice the difference in the spelling of the last name) was born January 17, 1916, and passed away on October 20, 1996. Minnie married Jacob Tiger, born on June 9, 1913, who died on April 9, 1993. Mary is buried in Star of David Memorial Park in North Lauderdale, Florida. Beatrice Mandell was born on December 8, 1919. Beatrice married Julius Pinsky on June 8, 1942. We know that Julius's mother's maiden name was Diamond. Julius passed on May 21, 2005. Beatrice and Julius' children are Edward and Bryna. Beatrice passed away on December 5, 2016, and is interred at Menorah Gardens in Southwest Ranches, Florida.

Finding information about Gussie proved to be challenging. I struggled at first to find the right Gussie. To start, different documents had multiple Gussie Cohens with similar dates of birth and places of death. Which one was correct? Census documents were more helpful. They provided a great deal of information. Gussie first appears in the 1915 New York State Census as born in Russia, not Poland, living as a lodger at 24 Norfolk Street in Manhattan. She was eighteen years old and had been in the United States for one year. Her occupation was an "Operator," which meant garment worker.

Each subsequent census added columns that gave more information. The 1920 Federal Census shows Gussie, her husband Alex, (who liked to call himself Eli), and their first two children, Minnie and Dorothy, still in Manhattan, at 204 Madison Street. Now, Gussie's birthplace is listed as Voliner, Russia. Another document lists her birthplace as Volhynia, Poland. Five years later, the family expanded as Gussie and Alex's two sons, Milton and Bernard, appeared in the 1925 New York State Census living at 263 New Lots Avenue in Brooklyn, with Gussie having emigrated to the United States in 1913. Now the family was close to their new delicatessen business.

The 1930 Federal Census tells us the Cohen Family moved again, this time to 339 Bedford Avenue, also in Brooklyn. The document also states that Gussie was married at seventeen. The 1940 Census shows that Alex was fifty-three and Gussie was forty-five. Daughter Minnie is no longer living with her parents, but now-married daughter Dorothy Margulis and her husband, Irving, are listed as living in the new home on South 3rd Street, with Milton and Bernard.

Even though not listed on the Census page, Milton said later on in an interview that the address was 327 South 3rd Street. Gussie's native language was recorded as Jewish. Gussie's husband, Alex Cohen (Chester), was born on July 15, 1886, in Belkrowova, Russia. He died on March 2, 1946, in The Bronx at fifty-nine years old. Going back a generation, Alex Cohen's parents were Hyman Cohen and his wife, Malka Kozak.

Both of Menachem's sons, Jack and Paul, were butchers by trade. Their naturalization papers state that their trade was butchering. Our grandfather, Milton, went to work for and with them in a butcher shop in the Bronx. Jack, Paul, and Milton told the same story about Menachem being gored by a bull. Family lore or truth?

My father never mentioned this "gored by a bull" story. What we have is passed down from family recollections. No one is around today to confirm any of it. I wish my father had mentioned some of these stories to me, but, unfortunately, he never shared them. All I can do is wonder why.

Paul Mandel was born in 1908 in Poland. He lived in the Bronx, where he owned and operated a Kosher butcher shop. His children were Sydell (Rona and Dona's mother) and Martin, my father's first cousins. Paul passed away on

July 28, 1983, at age seventy-five in Miami, Florida. Paul's brother, Jack, also worked in the butcher shop.

Finding information about Jack was much more challenging. Here's where the fun and frustration in research starts. According to the 1940 United States Federal Census, Jack (Yankel) Milnicer Mandel is listed as being born in Russia in 1902. This is probably Volin, Russia, though the document does not specify the town. A distant relative's family tree has him born in Shobeckova, Poland, in 1901. Other research lists Stebechve, Poland, as his birthplace in 1902. Stebechve was the Yiddish name for Volin or Volyn. Good luck finding the truth! The family has almost always accepted Stebechve, Poland, in 1902 as fact.

The Census says that Jack and his first wife, Rose Somovitz Mandel, lived at 3 St. Paul's Place in the Bronx, with their children Anna (Annie), age eleven, and Irving, listed as Milton (Milton was Irving's middle name), age five, both born in New York. Their children, Irving and Anna, were my father's first cousins. Jack died on January 30, 1989. He was married twice. His second wife was named Anna, which means he had a daughter named Anna, a sister named Anna, and a wife named Anna...lots of Annas on the family tree. Jack's daughter, Anna, is my Aunt Anna's (Jack's sister) niece. There are many Russian DNA links to my maternal and paternal sides. A large number of matches trace back to my Uncle Jack. Why this disproportionate amount? Maybe it has something to do with his two marriages?

Tillie Mandel was born on Christmas Day, December

25, and died in Florida on February 17, 1991. She was nine-ty-two and never married. Paul, Jack, Tillie, and Paul's wife, Betty, are interred in Lakeside Memorial Cemetery in Miami, Florida. Paul bought all the family plots.

Anna Mandel (Grandma Bertha's sister, not to be confused with Jack's daughter, Anna, or his second wife, Anna) married a man named Irving Fuchs (another Irving in the family). Anna and Irving had two daughters, Sheila and Mindy. Mindy lived in Brooklyn. Anna lived in Far Rockaway, New York, and sadly passed away on October 6, 2000. She is buried in New Montefiore Cemetery in West Babylon, New York. She was eighty-eight years old. Other descendants of the Mandel or Mandell branch of my family tree have chosen not to participate in this book and wish to remain anonymous. I have intentionally not used any information about them.

My paternal grandmother, Bertha Mandel Epstein, was born on April 10, 1906. She died on March 26, 1991, in Brooklyn, New York, at the age of eighty-four. She was a tailor. Her husband, Milton, predeceased her on July 4, 1954, at age fifty-four. He worked in a butcher store. Bertha and Milton were not affiliated with any societies and are buried in public ground at Mt. Hebron Cemetery in Kew Gardens, Queens, New York, near the World's Fair grounds in Flushing. As far as we know, Milton had two siblings, Lena and Morris. Morris is also buried in Mt. Hebron.

Milton's father, my great-grandfather, William Epstein, is also buried in Mt. Hebron. He was born on January 13, 1877, and passed away on September 16,

1939, at age sixty-two. William's wife, Rosie (Rosa), my great-grandmother, was born in 1874 and died on March 24, 1958, and was laid to rest in Beth Israel Cemetery in Woodbridge, New Jersey. She was eighty-four years old. Yes, husband and wife, William and Rosie, are in different cemeteries. My family would love to know why this happened. No one has given us a clear, provable answer. We have another mystery to be solved somewhere down the road.

Going back another generation, William's father, my great-great-grandfather, was Leib Epstein. Leib was married to a woman named Ida. Research has not discovered Ida's maiden name.

Researching great-grandma Yetta's family tree led to a relative who achieved great fame. Jan Peerce, the world-renowned opera tenor, was born on June 3, 1904, in New York City. His real name was Yehoshua Pinkhes Perelmuth (Jacob Pinkus Perelmuth), part of the Perelmuth (Perlmutter) branch of our family tree. According to one article, his headstone has a first name translated to Joshua. Jan's father, Louis, is my great-grandmother's uncle. This would make him a cousin. Louis and his wife, Henya Perelmuth, came from a small village, Horodetz, formerly in Poland, now part of Belarus.

As a young man, Jacob would often sing at family weddings and bar mitzvahs. This was confirmed by my cousins, Alex Chester, Alex Resnick, Rona, and Lois, who all heard of the talented singer from family stories passed down by their parents.

Jan Peerce starred at the Metropolitan Opera for twenty-seven years. He passed away in New Rochelle, New York, on December 15, 1984, at the age of eighty. Pictures of his headstone and footstone in Mount Eden Cemetery in Valhalla, New York, in Westchester County, are on Google.com.

My dad, Manny, loved to sing and was pretty good at it. Many times, his family told him that he resembled and sounded like Jan Peerce. Could this be DNA? Could it be nothing more than a coincidence? I wonder if there is a gene or chromosome that would lead one to have an interest in or be talented in music?

Although my father rarely discussed his relatives, he did tell me about another famous family member. I was told many times that the popular comedian, game show host, and actor, Jan Murray, born Murray Janofsky, was a distant relative. He was born in the Bronx on October 4, 1916, to Herman and Celia Janofsky, who emigrated from Eastern Europe.

Jan Murray became a famous Borscht Belt comedian starting in the 1930s. My dad said he was called "Tummler" in the Catskills. A "Tummler" was a jack-of-all-trades in the Borscht Belt. He would do stand-up comedy, act as an emcee and entertainment director—anything to keep the guests in a good mood.

Murray hosted numerous game shows on television, including *Treasure Hunt, Blind Date,* and *Dollar a Second,* to name a few. He also became a top headliner in Las Vegas, performing at the famous Flamingo Hotel on the Las Vegas

Strip. Murray made countless appearances on television programs such as *The Ed Sullivan Show, The Tonight Show,* and *The Joey Bishop Show.* Later in his career, he became a respected actor. Murray often raised money for charitable Jewish causes and entertained American soldiers as part of the USO (United Service Organizations) during World War II.

Jan Murray passed away on July 7, 2006, in Beverly Hills, California, at the age of eighty-nine. I sent an email to Jan's son, Howard, the acclaimed television director, who never wrote back. Maybe one day, I'll try again.

Other families that I am genetically connected to are the Gail Martineau family (a distant cousin with several connections) and the family of a woman named Julie Huneycutt, from Henderson, North Carolina, who has matching DNA at 132cM, even though she is not a biological child of her parents. Julie was adopted but still has matching DNA to her family. This story intrigues me, but when I spoke to Julie, she admitted there was shared DNA but didn't know where the connection was.

Julie Huneycutt is the adopted daughter of Herbert and Helen Halmovit Solomon. Herbert is the son of Saul and Helena (Lena) Epstein Solomon. Saul was born in Russia in 1895. Helena is my grandfather Milton's sister, my great-aunt. Growing up, we were told that Milton was an only child. It turns out that was not true. According to Ancestry.com, Helena was born in 1895 and died in 1981. My great-grandfather, William Epstein, was Helena's father. Confusing? I hope you took notes because there will be an open-book quiz next week.

The intrigue in this story is that Julie knows her birth mother was Elaine Wendy Friedman, also known as Wendy Elaine Friedman, from Colonial Heights, Virginia. Julie says the name is Wendy Elaine, but a document says Elaine Wendy. She was the daughter of Herbert and Helen Solomon. Herbert and Helen must have adopted their granddaughter, Julie! Elaine, who became a nurse, put Julie up for adoption at a young age. She later married Frank Robert Friedman and had another daughter, Jodi Lynn Friedman Woods.

What makes this case very unique is that I have a 132cM match to Julie, but my sister has only a 39cM match. Why is there such a difference? According to Ancestry, Julie is listed as a 2nd cousin once removed to me, but as a 4th cousin to my sister. DNA doesn't lie, but it can be incredibly confusing!

Having researched that, we come to the story of Jody Sandhaus, a Maryland woman with a DNA measurement of 165cM, which would make her a second cousin, or a second cousin half-removed on either the Mandel or Perlmutter branches of my family tree. Ancestry says Jody has DNA matches to my sister, my cousins Alex R., Rona, Dona, and Julie Huneycutt. None of us had ever heard of Jody before, but she's family now! According to Jody's husband, Doug, I am the highest DNA match to Jody that they have found! We have spoken two or three times, trying to determine the family connection. This is not an insignificant DNA match. Remember the phrase, "unanswered question?" Here's another one!

Digging deeper into DNA matches, there is also an interesting connection to a man named Anthony Howard, who has a centimorgan rating of 133. Biologically, he has to be a second cousin or half-second cousin, with roots in Scotland. According to Ancestry.com, he seems to come up on both sides of our family, but we cannot find any common ancestors. This remains a mystery, even though the cM level is high. An interesting genetic profile, to say the least.

Now, let's return to my Uncle Jack's family. I found on Ancestry a cousin named Jennifer Darer, with a DNA match of 144cM, which would make her a second cousin once removed or a half-first cousin, two times removed, who is on a branch of Jack's family tree. Jack and his wife, Rose, are Jennifer's great-grandparents, which means that either Irving (Milton) or Anna (Annie) had to be Jennifer's grandparent. Since we believe that Irving was never married nor had children, we must assume that Anna is Jennifer's grandmother. Family trees on Ancestry don't state this, but what else could it be? Isn't genealogical research fun?

Chapter 4

ANECDOTES AND MEMORIES

OUR GRANDMA BERTHA WAS INSTRUMENTAL in our love of Broadway and attending live performances. She took us to Radio City Music Hall back in the day, when you saw a feature film and a live show with the Radio City Rockettes. Lunch in a Manhattan restaurant was always a special treat, especially from Schrafft's and Lindy's. I developed my love of Strawberry Shortcake thanks to Grandma's lunches.

Our cousin, Rona, told me that her Grandma Betty took her and her sister, Dona, to Radio City as well. It's too bad we didn't know each other then, because the grandmothers and cousins could have attended together, sharing our love for food and entertainment.

Rona and Dona told me that every holiday was celebrated with their grandparents. Rona said, "We remember leaving our home on Long Island early in the day to make the four-hour trip to the Bronx. Our family celebrations centered around food, but the time we spent with our grandparents will always be treasured. All types of aromas would greet us when we visited. After the long trip, we couldn't wait to eat!"

Rona and her sister, Dona, told me that their grandmother cooked all the time. Their holidays, especially the Jewish holidays, were more memorable because their grandmother added the special ingredient of love into her cooking, making the celebrations stand out. Their Grandma Betty's made-from-scratch gefilte fish was a highlight of the family meal. Rona and Dona feel almost the same way about their mother, Sydell, and her cooking. A pinch of this or that made every day and meal more delightful.

Another story that Rona shared involved her grandma, Betty, and Rona's daughter, Tracy. "When Tracy didn't want to eat the salmon that her grandmother prepared, Betty knew that Tracy loved anything and everything pink, so Grandma Betty told my daughter that the salmon was pink chicken," Rona recalled. "Tracy loved her pink chicken. Grandma loved to make chunky applesauce with rhubarb. It was her signature dessert. Since it was pink, Tracy loved it."

Rona also shared that her mother, Sydell, made a great noodle pudding. She said it was so delicious that you could eat it for breakfast, lunch, dinner, or a late-night snack. Many people asked for the recipe, but Sydell didn't give it out, claiming it was a secret family recipe. An explosion of flavors awaited everyone when Sydell made her favorite recipes. She took her time perfecting her craft, and her family loved what she did.

Dona shared two stories of her mother's specialties. "My mom took sweet potatoes after they were cooked, put them in the broiler, which was the bottom part of the stove, then poured honey on them and made candied sweet potatoes. I also remember her making sweet and sour cabbage soup. I was her official soup taster to see if it needed more sweet or sour."

Grandma Bertha was a fabulous cook. She could have been a professional chef if she wanted to be. Grandma never wrote down her recipes. Everything was in her head as she created incredible, unique flavors. Her pot roast and potato kugel were to die for. I have vivid memories of Grandma Bertha's kugel. To see something similar on a dinner table today brings me back to those special meals. If you've ever tasted her delicious apple rugelach, believe me, you'd remember it!

Grandma always knew how to develop flavors, but not necessarily with spice. There wasn't much she couldn't do using the right amounts of salt, pepper, oil, and butter. To me, that culinary knowledge makes for a fantastic cook! When my husband ate Grandma's food for the first time, he immediately said Bertha's cooking reminded him of his grandmother's. I love to cook and so wish I had Grandma Bertha's culinary knowledge.

Our Grandma Bertha always cooked for the family Thanksgiving celebration. The holiday would not be complete without a delicious roast turkey with stuffing, kugel, fresh-baked rolls, and a selection of her favorite tasty delights for dessert. Sadly, she stopped this tradition when my dad, her son, passed away. Although my family has created new holiday traditions, Thanksgiving will never be the same.

As part of our celebrations, many of us cherish the handwritten recipes of our parents and grandparents—a box of recipes on index cards tucked away on a kitchen shelf or faded papers in a binder. Our grandparents and aunts had those or something similar. Oh, the secrets those documents stored! All it took was a pinch of this, an extra shake of that, and the use of a brand-name product instead of a generic brand to create aromas and tastes that stayed with us forever. A delicious smell can trigger long-lost memories of food, laughter, tears, and smiles at the kitchen or dining room table. What an honor it was if an ancestor let you help in any way, creating these loving memories.

Everyone in my family agrees that the food we grew up with, the comfort foods of our past, connected us to our ancestors. Sharing these delicious memories with the next generation only heightens our recollections of the foods and relatives of years ago. When they came to America from Eastern Europe, many of our ancestors brought the recipes and traditions of the old world. Dishes that originated in the mother country as a necessity found new life in the United States as a luxury when served on special occasions and holidays.

Naturally, the prices of these delicacies have gone up. Have you seen the price of "Kasha Varnishkes" (bow tie noodles and kasha, cooked with chopped sauteed onions) on a kosher delicatessen menu? Outrageous! I make it at home. My husband and neighbors devour it! While several of these recipes and dishes are not the healthiest by today's standards, it is still up to us to preserve these delights.

Two ingredients heavily used years ago, but not as much today, are schmaltz (rendered chicken fat) and lard (rendered pork fat). Both of these items were used in frying and baking, adding flavor to the dish. Schmaltz was commonly found in Ashkenazi Jewish cooking in many of the recipes brought over from Eastern Europe. I know for a fact that my Grandma Bertha regularly used schmaltz. She didn't use lard because it came from a pig, but used Crisco, a vegetable shortening, as a substitute, especially in her desserts.

Cooking and food were common themes in the family. Great-Aunt Gussie, aka Jean Chester (when she moved to California, she felt her married name, Cohen, sounded too Jewish, so she changed it to Chester), also had a special flair in the kitchen. Gussie had a business head, so she combined cooking, her lifelong passion for food, and business, opening a "kolbasnya," better known as a delicatessen, in New York.

Gussie and her husband, Alexander, owned delis in New York. They fed many people who were facing hunger and had the cleanest delis anywhere, because those they fed cleaned the stores in return for the food. Their homemade knishes, meat, chicken, and vegetable dishes were all made from scratch. Family stories have said that Gussie and Alexander's delicious potato and kasha knishes rivaled those made at Yonah Schimmel's, the world-famous knishery on East Houston Street on the Lower East Side of Manhattan.

No family recipes were ever written down or shared with anyone in the family. Other family members have searched for written copies of Gussie's recipes with no success. The secrets to her scrumptious gastronomical goodies are gone forever. Her family has praised her culinary body of work for years. We all wish there were a Grandma Gussie's cookbook. It would be a bestseller!

Gussie and Alex's generosity and philanthropy were well-known to their family and friends. In addition to providing free food for members of their community who were in need, they contributed to charities in and out of their community. This was during the Great Depression and after the Stock Market Crash.

The need and will to survive were in Gussie's DNA. She found a way to make a living and support her family. Overcoming her early-life struggles was inherent in her, and she created a business presence in the community. Gussie's struggles led to her strength as an adult and businesswoman. Her spirit and drive to succeed were nothing short of honorable. Working with family is difficult, but Gussie's clan made it work because they had to. Everyone chipped in to make the machine run. Failure wasn't an option.

Gussie's grandsons told me about her effervescent personality and how amazing she was. Even though I met her when I was young, I don't remember much about her other than that she resembled our Grandma Bertha.

Gussie's son, Bernard (Bernie), and his wife, Irene, owned and operated a luncheonette/soda fountain/candy store, "The Roxy," located on Broadway, the main drag, near the old Broadway Theater, in Monticello, New York, in Sullivan County. Bernie made the most amazingly delicious egg creams, ice cream sodas, thick shakes, and malteds. Alex C. said that Bernie's vanilla malteds were the best he had ever tasted. I'm craving one right now, just thinking about it. Again, food runs in the family! My cousins raved about Bernie's creations. Can there be too much of a good thing? Not in this restaurant!

Next door to The Roxy on one side was the Monticello Short Line Bus Station and the Playland Arcade. On the other side was the old Davco Store, now the Monticello Public Library (Ethelbert B. Crawford Public Library at 479 Broadway). The people of Monticello voted in 2012 to buy and renovate the old Davco Building. The Roxy's location brought in a lot of customers, especially from New York City, for their all-inclusive Catskill Mountains vacations. The luncheonette had a huge lunch business during the high-octane summer months, serving a large array of sandwiches, burgers, and fries, mostly prepared by Bernie.

During these times, the Catskills had numerous resorts (Grossinger's, Brown's, The Concord, The Raleigh, The Nevele, and Kutcher's, just to name a few) filled with New Yorkers escaping the heat and humidity of Gotham for the cooler temperatures of the mountains. Today, on the grounds of the former Concord resort stands Resorts World Catskills, a hotel and casino. The famed Monster

Golf Course is still there. When I was younger, I had been to Kerhonkson, New York, in Ulster County, close to Monticello, to visit my mother's family, but I knew nothing about my Monticello family.

Bernie, a veteran of World War II, passed away in hospice care on January 2, 2008, in Boca Raton, Florida, at the age of eighty-two. He was a member of the *Workmen's Circle*. His wife, Irene, died on May 28, 2011, also in Boca Raton at eighty-four years of age. She previously worked for the New York State Department of Labor.

Andrew Jacobs, the President of the Catskills Borscht Belt Museum Board of Directors in Ellenville, New York, told me that he remembered Bernie, Irene, and their store. Andrew and his fellow members are searching through their archives and reaching out to others for photographs and documents. One photograph was suggested by my cousin, Stewart Chester. The picture came from the Arcadia Press book, *Images of America*, published in 2010. Tom Rue is credited for the photo. The picture is on Google and Facebook.

The Catskills Institute, associated with Northeastern University in Boston, Massachusetts, doesn't have any photos of or documents relating to The Roxy. They wished me well in my search and asked for copies of anything I might find. The search continues!

My cousins told me stories of visiting their Grandma Gussie in Monticello, but I never knew she lived there until recently. Her house still stands today. Her grandson, my cousin Alex Resnick, knows where it is located on Route 42

(Forestburg Road). I'll definitely pass by the next time I'm in the Catskills.

Many who traveled by car to and from the Catskills stopped off at the historic, now demolished, Red Apple Rest on Route 17 in Tuxedo, New York. The Red Apple Rest was a popular stop-off point for the travelers, especially when the trip took four to five hours to drive from the city. I remember eating there with my husband in the 1980s when the restaurant was a dated, worn-down version of its former glory. Good food for lunch was served with a plate-ful of memories of the restaurant's golden days. You could tell then that the famed restaurant's days were numbered.

Another noted restaurant stopping point in Sullivan County was and is the Roscoe Diner on Old Route 17 in the famous fishing hamlet of Roscoe, New York. The Roscoe Diner is still in business, serving delicious meals seven days a week. I remember being there a few times while traveling through the area. I had a hot open turkey sand-wich the last time I was there.

My California cousins are all descended from Gussie and Alexander. Their daughter, Minnie, had three children, Sharon, Lester, and Alex R. Minnie inherited her mother's talent for cooking. Alex R. said that his mom was the defi-nition of a "Jewish mother" or a "Jewish grandmother." Food, cooking, and forgotten family recipes now reached the West Coast. The California clan has now expanded to include many members of the Rosenblum Family.

Gussie's other grandson, Alex Chester, told me that his mother, Florence, was an "okay cook," but not all that inventive or eclectic. Florence had several recipes she was quite good at, such as brisket, spaghetti and meatballs, stuffed cabbage, and soups. She would prepare dishes that her family loved. The dinner menu was repeated every week or every other week. She didn't make many exotic dishes, preferring her tried and true favorites, but she always served a selection of culinary delights for the family Thanksgiving banquet.

Alex R. raved about his mother's cooking. "My mom (Minnie) cooked all of the Jewish foods... chopped liver, chopped herring, brisket, stuffed cabbage, meat loaf with sweet potatoes, eggs with lox, onions and peas, latkes, chicken salad, stuffed kishka (a sausage and stuffing combination cooked in some type of casing), cutlets, and of course, chicken soup. Every meal was a holiday." Alex R. added that when his mom made the family Thanksgiving meal, it was like a dinner on steroids. "She was a very creative cook. For other holidays like Passover, Hanukkah, and Rosh Hashanah, guests always celebrated with us. Family and friends celebrated together. It was lots of fun at the dining table."

Uncle Paul Mandel owned and operated a butcher shop, Paul Mandel Meat and Poultry Market, located at 570 West 235th Street in the Riverdale section of the Bronx. It was a major source of income for the family. Paul learned the skill and artistry of butchery from his father, Menachem. Kosher food at its best! Their customers loved them. The advertisement shared here (see documents) comes from the 1960 edition of *Neighborhood Directory*, which advertised local businesses in the Fieldston, Riverdale, and Spuyten Duyvil sections of The Bronx. Many thanks to Janet Munch, the Special Collections Librarian at Lehman College, for all her help in finding this long-lost advertisement... part of my family's hidden history.

Uncle Paul and Aunt Betty resided at 3900 Greystone Avenue in the Bronx, in an apartment building near the campus of Manhattan University. Rona said that when she was young, the shape of the building looked like a castle. Paul and Betty could easily walk from their apartment to the butcher shop. Uncle Paul owned the butcher shop for many years before selling the business to one of his long-time employees, Ernie, who changed the name of the business to Ernie's Kosher Meats and Poultry, staying in the same location for years.

According to my friend, Vivian Scrocca, who grew up in the Bronx, "Back then, where the market was, was all Italian and Jewish. It was a great neighborhood." A Dunkin' Donuts shop stands today where the market was. There is also a strong Russian-American community in and around Riverdale. Could this be one of the reasons why Uncle Paul chose to live and own a business there?

Chapter 5

STEBECHVE... OUR ANATEVKA

THE AWARD-WINNING MUSICAL *FIDDLER ON the Roof* is one of the greatest shows in the history of Broadway theater. The book was written by Joseph Stein, with music by Jerry Bock and lyrics by Sheldon Harnik. The story is based on *Tevye the Dairyman,* written by the Russian author and playwright Sholem Aleichem.

Fiddler takes place in a village (shtetl) called Anatevka around the year 1905 in what was called the "Pale of Settlement," a part of Western Russia where most Jews were forced to live after being forbidden to live in other regions. Nowadays, the "Pale" would cover all of Belarus and Moldova, and parts of Ukraine, Poland, Lithuania, Latvia, and Russia.

The lead character is Tevye the Milkman, who wants to observe his Jewish traditions and life. He does not like the changing world he must deal with. The song that ends the play is called *Anatevka,* where Tevye and the villagers lament that they must leave their cherished home.

My ancestors' Anatevka, their Eastern European shtetl home for decades, was a place called Stebechve. I had never heard of the place until research on Ancestry.com led me to a distant cousin, Jake Garfinkle, who wrote his 2023 Undergraduate Honors Thesis at Brown University in Providence, Rhode Island, about Jews in Stebechve. His thesis is entitled, *An Autoethnography of Stebechve: Jewish Community Burial, and Memory through Diaspora in New York.*

I might not have discovered an important part of my family tree if it weren't for Jake and his thesis. Jake unlocked a door that my cousins and I knew nothing about. His work has now given our family another chance to look at a distant part of our history... a part previously unknown to many today, but one firmly connected to my roots. I have Jake's permission to use part of his thesis, and I thank him for it.

Jake and I are distantly related through his Tinter Family. Jake's DNA match to me was a mere 13cM, which, according to Ancestry.com, makes him anywhere between a fifth and eighth cousin on my father's side. The Tinter Family's ancestors were from Stebechve. Therefore, somewhere back in time, my family and Jake's family shared a common ancestor, but we don't know who it is.

Quite often, a low DNA match results in little to no information, but in this case, I hit the jackpot with Jake. When I reached out via email through Ancestry.com, he responded quickly. I asked him, "How could my great-aunt and uncle be on your tree?" He told me, "They came from Stebechve, and you probably didn't know about it." That's when he told me about his thesis.

Jake's thesis research discovered that my Great-aunt Bella's married last name was Springer. Our family had been looking under her maiden name, Miliciner, then later, Mandel. Jake's research opened a long-closed door.

We didn't know that Bella was married and that her surname was Springer. Her brother, Paul, my great-uncle, knew about Bella's marriage and name change. Paul was the person who reported the information about Bella and Josef to Yad Vashem (see document from Chapter Three).

Stebechve was the Yiddish name of the shtetl in Volyn, in the northwest section of Ukraine. The Jews of this town chose Stebechve as the name of the place where they came from. Stebechve is now called Stobykhva. It has also been called Stobychwa (the Polish name of the town), Stobechow, and Soberwa. The town is located twenty-four miles east-northeast of Kovel and nineteen miles south-southwest of Kamin-Kashyrskyi (also known as Stobykhra).

Stebechve was in the Pale of Settlement in the western reaches of the Russian Empire, an impoverished area where Jews were segregated and forced to live in poverty. The area was also a center for Jewish culture and the Yiddish language. According to the thesis, the Jewish population of Stebechve is documented as dating back to the mid-1800s, but they were probably there before.

When controlled by Russia, the Polish name of Volyn became Volhynia, as evident in United States Census documents. This is proof that whichever country won a military battle controlled the naming rights of the town.

Fighting during World War I took place in and around Stebechve. The deaths of many German soldiers killed in action in Stebechve after attacking the Russian army are recorded on Ancestry.com.

Jake's research helped us uncover the fates of our great-aunt and uncle, Bella and Josef Springer, as well as their children, who all perished in the Holocaust. Their "crime" was being Jews at the wrong time and place. Under German Fascist rule, Jews were considered enemies of the State, the lowest of the low, while Adolf Hitler's Third Reich called themselves the Master Race.

Jewish-owned businesses were taken over by the Nazis or destroyed by fire. Kristallnacht, also known as the Night of Broken Glass, took place throughout Germany on November 9 and 10, 1938. Jewish-owned homes, businesses, schools, and synagogues were severely vandalized, with Jewish men arrested and then sent to concentration camps. This was no longer just an economic and political event. Life had now turned violent. Some people consider this event the beginning of the Holocaust.

It is well documented that across Europe, over six million Jews were killed in the Holocaust, with more than two and a half million dying in the Nazi death camps. This was the political and social climate that scores of Jews, including some of my ancestors, faced before coming to America, if they were lucky enough to do so.

While the landscape and politics of Stebechve have changed, the fact remains that it is the historical home of my paternal ancestors. The anti-Semitism and violence experienced by my ancestors were real. Much of it continues to this day. The effects of the Holocaust and pogroms cannot be denied. Violence committed against Jews by Russians, Poles, and Germans led to increased immigration to the United States, in particular New York City, where they felt safe. Many immigrant families immediately settled in Manhattan's Lower East Side, where they lived in overcrowded, unhealthy tenements. Those who deny what happened are wrong, and their denials must be challenged every time.

Over the years, the Brighton Beach section of Brooklyn, often called "Little Odessa," has become the center of Russian-American and Ukrainian-American life in New York. Many Eastern European immigrants who arrived in New York came to live here and in the surrounding areas of Coney Island, Manhattan Beach, Midwood, and Sheepshead Bay. To this day, the neighborhood continues as a hotbed of Eastern European culture in New York, with restaurants, shopping, and festivals. It is one of the largest Russian communities in the United States. If you take a walk along Brighton Beach Avenue from Coney Island Avenue to Ocean Parkway, you'll see a world unlike any other. There are also flourishing Russian-American communities in Forest Hills and Rego Park in Queens.

The current conflict between Russia and Ukraine has divided parts of Brooklyn, with supporters on both sides; however, a casual look indicates greater support for Ukraine, with bright blue and yellow flags displayed in houses and businesses. Most Russians in the communities are opposed to the current Russian government. Trust and the Russian government seem to be mutually exclusive in these communities.

Other immigrants from the former Soviet Union chose to live on the West Coast, creating and developing large communities in San Francisco and Los Angeles, bringing with them unique customs, traditions, and foods, while escaping poverty, as well as religious and political persecution. Just imagine the grit and determination these immigrants had, leaving their homeland to come to a new country to start their lives all over again. How brave these people were to cross the Atlantic Ocean with literally little more than the clothes on their backs!

Many of the emigrants from Stebechve came to the United States and settled in New York. They formed a *Landsmanshaft,* or Jewish Society, *Chevra Beth David Anshe Stebechve.* The word "Landsmanshaft" comes from a German and Yiddish derivation meaning "association of compatriots." Quoting from Jake's thesis, "The primary function of the Landsmanshaft was to facilitate communal burial of Stebechve Jews." The thesis continued, "The whole family is buried together among other 'landsleit,' or people from the same place in the old country." For the emigrants, it was a life of continuous challenges for children and adults.

The Landsmanshaft organizations would be used for social and philanthropic purposes. You could call it a mutual aid society or hometown society of Jewish immigrants from the same European town or village, working together to form their communal burial location. Most of the Landsmanshafts were created in the late nineteenth or early twentieth centuries. It was part of the immigrant experience. At one point in time, they numbered in the thousands across the country. Today, the number of active Societies has been drastically reduced. Original members of the Societies are long gone, but some of their descendants are still with us.

When doing research, gravestones can provide a valuable source of information to those who wish to research their family trees. Jewish gravestones, especially older ones, often have information written in Hebrew, which might require the use of someone who can read the language. Names (especially the father of the deceased), dates, and places might be found on the markers.

Jewish cemeteries have people who work with them as facilitators/representatives of the different Societies. Jake Garfinkle is now a facilitator/representative of the *Chevra Beth David Anshe Stebechve Society* for Beth David Cemetery in Elmont, New York. Many of the older societies no longer have these facilitators/representatives as the eldest members of the societies, and their descendants are no longer with us.

Many of our relatives and other villagers are buried in Beth David Cemetery. Additional paternal relatives are part of a different Society, *Workmen's Circle*, and are buried in Mount Hebron Cemetery in Flushing, New York. Other Stebechve "Landsmen" are interred in Washington

Cemetery in Brooklyn, New York. My maternal Grandfather, Louis Kaplan, always talked about his "Landsmen," but never explained what that was. Thanks to Jake, I now understand what my grandfather was talking about.

Grampa Lou belonged to the *Chevra B'Nei Rabbi Menachem Anshe Dubrowa Society.* As part of his responsibilities in his Society, he was a "Hospitaler," someone who visited fellow Society members when they were hospitalized. Grampa was born on March 5 or March 7 in Kiev in 1894. Records say that he was born on the seventh, but Grampa insisted he was born on the fifth, so our family always celebrated his birthday on the fifth. Grampa was a tailor. He passed away on January 23, 1981, at age eighty-six, almost three months after I was married. As the family elder, he blessed the bread at my wedding reception. I still remember him as proud as can be in his pinstripe suit and red tie. Grampa bought all of our family plots at Beth David Cemetery, where he was laid to rest.

I read Jake's thesis as if it were a best-selling historical novel. At first, I knew nothing about Stebechve, but with each succeeding page, I felt as if I was there, in that time. My love of history drew me to the story. The fact that my family was part of this story made it more compelling. I have long been a fan of and appreciative of academia, academic research, and scholarship. The effort that goes into a strong, descriptive thesis illustrates the hard work and long hours needed to create such a piece. The depth and scope of Jake's thesis were impressive. His narrative of the tangled life of the people of Stebechve brought the reader back in time as if they were living then, from the refugees' immigration to the United States, bringing their culture and experiences to their new lives in New York.

Jake... Ya done good! I am eternally grateful! You've become a hero to my family and me for what you've given us. Long-lost family members have come back to us thanks to your research. My family and I may not have the full picture of events from years ago, but we certainly have a fuller picture.

Chapter 6

FAMILY STORIES

WHILE RESEARCHING MY FAMILY, THEN finally meeting their descendants, I found that I was not the only one who wanted to learn more about the people who were here before us. I asked my cousins to share some stories and memories of relatives I was first learning about. What follows are segments of those family tales that brought me closer to people I had barely or never known. Cousin Alex Resnick starts with a few memories of his family.

Gussie (Jean) Cohen Chester #1

I loved my Grandmother Gussie. She was always treating me with kindness. She loved to pick blueberries, then bake pies, cupcakes, and sometimes make blueberry pancakes using the bounty she had just picked. I can still taste her delicious creations. As I grew a little older (maybe five or six years old), she taught me how to play cards. She loved playing gin rummy and poker. She also loved to gamble.

I remember when the Monticello Racetrack opened in 1958

with harness racing. Grandmother loved to go to the track. I was eight years old at the time, and we became Daily Double partners. I gave her a dollar and gave her two numbers for her to bet, 7-2.

The next morning at breakfast, my grandmother opened her purse and had a stack of twenty-dollar bills. Both horses won, were long shots, and my share of the winnings was one hundred and sixty dollars. I can still hear my mother arguing with Grandma that "You don't give an eight-year-old one hundred and sixty dollars cash!" and my Grandma telling my mother, "Alex's numbers won three hundred and twenty dollars!" Mom let me keep ten dollars, then my dad took me to the bank and opened a savings account for me. I always thought I had the best grandma ever.

Gussie (Jean) Cohen Chester # 2

In May of 1966, I was very tired. I had just finished my last round of six final exams at the UCLA School of Business. I was set to graduate in eight days after my last final exam. I decided I was going to skip the graduation ceremony and go camping to rest and relax in the great outdoors. My mother then told me that Grandmother Gussie was flying to Los Angeles to attend the graduation.

Grandma arrived and talked me into driving her to Las Vegas, where we could both rest for three or four days, then return to Los Angeles and attend the graduation. I gave in, and the next day we left for Vegas.

We checked into the hotel/casino at 6 PM, rested for a while, then went to one of the restaurants in the hotel for a nice dinner. After dinner, we left the restaurant, and I started walking to the elevator. Grandma Gussie turned the other way, headed straight towards the casino. I figured that she was confused, so I turned back to her and said, "Grandma, the room is this way." She said, "I know, but the casino is this way!"

I went upstairs to sleep. Grandma went and played the nickel slot machines. She returned to the room about 1 AM with two buckets filled with nickels. We both had a fun trip.

It seems as if my Aunt Gussie was quite the character. Many family stories have been passed down about her. Aunt Gussie never moved to California, but visited every year, staying for four months. Retired by the time her family moved to California in the 1950s, she was an early jet-setter, traveling between New York, Florida, and California. According to her grandsons, she was a hoot! ... lots of fun and always happy.

Alex Resnick then shared more stories about his mother, Minnie, father Harry, and Great-Grandmother, Yetta.

Minnie Chester Resnick # 1

My mother, Minnie, was thoughtful and kind. She was also brave and quick to defend those whom she loved. Two examples: The first was around 1950 in Monticello, during a very cold winter. My brother, Lester, came home from school with a letter from his teacher. My mother couldn't read the letter because of the poor penmanship. The next morning, my mother dressed me in warm clothing, then my sister, brother, Mom, and I waited for the school bus. We lived about three miles out of town, and my mother didn't drive. We arrived at school, where everything was okay until my brother's teacher translated the letter. The letter said, "Lester needs to improve his poor penmanship." You can guess the rest! It became a classic family story.

Minnie Chester Resnick # 2

We moved to Los Angeles in 1960. When I was about eighteen years old, in my second year at UCLA, my mother asked me to drive her to an appointment. On the way to her appointment, I did not see a temporary "No Left Turn" sign. A police officer saw me and issued me my first-ever ticket after I turned left.

My mother told me not to pay the ticket fine because there was no reason for the temporary sign. She wanted to go to court and fight the ticket. My mom and I drove to downtown L.A. for Traffic Court a few months later. We had to wait over two hours for our turn with the judge.

I'm standing in front of the judge, and my mother is sitting in the witness area. The judge reads the ticket to me and asks how I plead. I say, "Guilty, your Honor," then, in a split second, my mother jumps up and says, "Not guilty, your honor!"

The judge calls Mom up to the bench, tells her that it is not her ticket, and she needs to let the judge do his job. The judge asks me again how I plead. While I say, "Guilty," my mother says, "Not guilty!" By then, everyone in the courtroom, even the judge, is howling. The judge finds me guilty, fines me eighty dollars, and tells my mother that she needs to let me pay my fine. My mother opens her purse, pulls out a stack of twenty-dollar bills, and tries to hand them to the judge.

On the drive home, my mother and I couldn't stop laughing.

She's lucky the judge didn't throw her in jail!

Harry Resnick

My father, Harry Resnick, was a generous and loving man. He was a businessman for nearly all of his adult life. When I was born in 1945, he already owned two auto dealerships in Monticello, New York. He also leased a parking lot from the Pennsylvania Railroad in Downtown Manhattan. He had a thirty-day lease and stayed for twenty-four years. My birth certificate lists my father's occupation as "parking lot owner."

When we moved to Los Angeles in 1960, my father purchased a dry cleaning and laundry business. He built the business to multiple locations to feed a central plant. I later used the same model to restructure my own printing business in the 1970s to 1990s.

Dad was always available to support me as a child, teenager, college student, and as an adult. I learned so much from him.

Alex Resnick's parents, Harry and Minnie, moved to California, leaving behind the snow, ice, shoveling, and brutally cold weather of Monticello and the Catskill Mountains. Southern California in the 1960s and 1970s was like heaven... affordable and not crowded. Many relatives and friends visited them. Alex's father's brother chose a mixed climate when he moved... he moved to Chicago.

Yetta Meeninyeetza Mandel

My mother once took me to visit her grandmother, Yetta. I was about four or five years old and hadn't started school yet. This was in 1949 or 1950 in Monticello. My mother explained to me that Yetta didn't speak any English, instructing me to smile at Yetta if she spoke to me. I did just that. When we got to Yetta's house, she was sitting in a rocking chair. She looked old but happy that we were visiting her. Seventy-five years after meeting my great-grandmother, I have nothing but love and respect for her.

The more I hear about my long-gone relatives, the more I wish I could have met them. I know there are other family members out there. Thinking about those I've met only encourages me to keep searching for more. I understand that some family members wish to remain private and not have their lives opened up. Out of respect for their privacy, I do not mention them... but I have found you. I wish that someday we could meet, so I can learn more about you and our family. I would fervently hope that our ancestors agree.

Chapter 7

ALEX CHESTER INTERVIEWS HIS GRANDMA GUSSIE

INTERVIEWING RELATIVES IN AN ORAL history is a fabulous way of learning about the past and preserving memories for the future. Some families have old audio cassettes of family histories and interviews. If they are lucky, some families have VHS tapes. Both of those technologies are wonderful, but over time, the tapes may deteriorate, either damaging or destroying the precious information and secrets they hold. Try finding a VHS machine nowadays when you need it. For some, it's nearly impossible.

Transferring those recorded stories to newer technologies in our digital world, while still preserving the old ones, is a must. Future generations should see and hear everything possible about their lineage... and the stories that go with it. History cannot die simply because we live in a different century. Having said that, any handwritten document is precious, especially if the writer is a family member. A box of sheet protectors can go a long way in preserving essential legal documents, family recipes, poems, and stories.

Cousin Alex Chester shared an interview that he, his ex-wife, Carol, and his father, Milton, conducted with his Grandma Gussie when she was seventy-eight years old. Some of Gussie's recollections in the interview may not match historical documents, but these were her memories. We could attribute this to time, aging, or a creative mind. We simply don't know.

Gussie Mandel Cohen (Jean Chester) emigrated to the United States aboard the S.S. Finland, which sailed from Antwerp, Belgium, on January 4, 1913, arriving in America on January 16. She passed away on May 10, 1980, at eighty-two years of age. Gussie is buried in Wellwood Beth Moses Cemetery in West Babylon, New York. Cemetery records incorrectly list her age at her death as seventy-one. She was a member of the *Adath Israel of Brooklyn* Society. Here is part of a transcript of the interview with Gussie. She talks about her memories of life in Europe and starting a business in New York.

C: How old are you?

G: *Seventy-eight years old.*

C: You're seventy-eight?

G: *Believe it or not.*

A: That means you must have been born in 1898.

G: *I think so. 1898? What's the difference? A year more. A year less. But this is what I am.*

A: Where were you born?

G: *In Russia.*

C: What part of Russia?

G: *That's important? Vayinskagabirnya.*

A: Can you spell that? (Laughter)

G: *No! (Laughter) Where did I start? This isn't really the start.*

M: It's called the province of Valinska.

G: *Kievkoveljelesnadaroga. (General laughter) Yeah, yeah. It sounds funny, but it's...*

M: That's Kiev.

G: *Kiev! That's a very big...*

A: Is that the Ukraine?

G: *Yeah. Ukraine.*

M: K-I-E-V, the capital of the Ukraine.

C: Is it near there?

G: *No. That's where it is, you call it. It's part of Russia.*

A: Were you born in the city of Kiev?

G: *Around. Around.*

C: Around. In the countryside? Out in the country?

G: *Yeah. Yeah. Smaller town.*

A: Was it a village?

G: *Yeah. It was a village. Stabuchvah (Stebechve). Nah, it's not nothing! You can say Covey. It's easier to spell. And that's where we were. Fifteen miles away from there. And there you have the transportation... thirty-two changes a day.*

C: Trains that went through?

G: *Yeah. And the Russian czar, when they opened up*

that place. The Russian czar came to see it.

A: What was the name? Covella?

G: *Not Covella. Kovel.*

C: What was your mother like? What was her maiden name and do you know any of her family?

G: *Yeah. Her name was Perlmutter. She also lost her father when she was very young. They were two sisters. That's all. My grandmother was a very good businesswoman. I think I took after her.*

C: Did you know her sister? Did you know your aunt?

G: *I knew her sister. Sure. Now they're not alive. I knew her sister and I knew my grandmother. I always liked to travel. Before I went to America, I went to say goodbye to them, and they didn't live in the town where I was.*

C: Where did they live?

G: *They lived in a different town. (Laughter)*

C: Do you remember their names?

G: *Sure! (Laughter) My grandma's name was... they used to call her Shanedella Demelechka, because she had a... he was a... years back they were very religious, so the husband used to sit and doven and pray, and the wife was the business lady. So I'm taking, I took after my grandmother Shanedella. They used to call her Shanedella Demelechka because she sold flour and spices and all that. Well, she was a very witty woman. She...*

C: She was like the Miller.

G: What kind of Miller?

C: They have to do with flour.

G: But a miller is not with flour, and grits, and you know, for cereals.

C: And did you know your grandfather?

G: No. My mother didn't even remember him. Yeah. And she was the older one. Oh there is a lot of, you know, in a family there's a lot of... My aunt, her sister, was hit by thunder.

C: Hit by lightning?

G: Yeah. The lightning. And she was all colored up, like burns to her face and everything.

C: She was lucky she lived through it.

G: Yeah. She lived quite a while, until Hitler, I suppose, came.

C: What was your aunt's name? Your mother's sister.

G: Ah, just one minute. I think Bella. Just a minute. I was there saying goodbye before I went to America. I think Bella was her name. Yeah. Bella. I had a sister, Bella, too. Bella, yeah. That's right. That was her name. And she had children and, but she was it. It was funny, you know, they got... they were surprised that she remained alive because she was all marked up from the burns. Yeah, but they were wealthy. He was also in the same line like cattle and all that. So they used to send her in the summer to the countries, and they took care of her... My father had brothers. I remember my grandfather, my grandmother. Sure.

C: Did your father have brothers and sisters?

G: *Yeah.*

C: Did you know them?

G: *Wait a minute! Sisters? I don't remember whether he had sisters. I think they were all brothers. They must have been maybe six brothers, for sure. I remember my grandfather. My grandmother too.*

C: What was your grandfather's name?

G: *Ben Yehudin. That's Bernard, it's a name after his. Bernard is the name.*

C: How do you spell it?

G: *Whatever you spell it, you'll read it. It's Hebrew. Bernard is the name. Yeah, Bernard David.*

C: David was his last name?

G: *No, not the last name. Their last name was Mandel. That was two names. Melnyeetza (Meeninyeetza), that's in Russia. In Russia it was Melnyeetza (Meeninyeetza). When we came here, it became Mandel. Yeah. You see, when we came here, my... The reason that it became Mandel so fast is that my sister, Mary, married a cousin, you know, and his name was a brother of my father. You know what Pop's name was? Papa Alex.*

The more I learn about my Aunt Gussie, the more I want to discover, not just from a historical or culinary perspective, but also learning about what kind of person she was. Could we call her strong-willed? Undoubtedly. Her incredible determination to succeed left an everlasting impression on her family and descendants. Could you call her an early feminist? Quite possibly. A courageous advocate for her family? Without a doubt! Gussie certainly had a mind of her own and was not afraid to speak her truth. Undeniably, she cared about people, especially her family, working long days and nights with her husband and children to create a successful business and become a special presence in the community.

Out of all the "discoveries" of my family, Gussie was the most intriguing. Coming from a world of despair and near poverty, she remade herself into a respected entrepreneur, matriarch, and success story. She refused to accept the status quo, changing what could likely have been a completely different fate.

Another interesting tidbit Alex shared about Gussie is that she always wore pearls. It was rare to find a picture of her without them. You could say pearls were part of Gussie's "uniform." When Gussie passed away, Alex's wife, Sherry, inherited some pearls from Gussie. Because of her penchant for wearing pearls, we think the woman accompanying my great-great-grandmother, Yetta, down the aisle at my parents' wedding is Gussie, but we're not sure.

After speaking with Gussie's descendants, it was clear that the glowing flame of her passion for taking care of her family and business inspired others in the family to succeed. Her presence and drive in the business community and her strength as the family matriarch at the same time were admirable and notable. If you're wondering if Gussie was eccentric... well... I did too! Her long-term memories may have been affected by time, but her passion never died.

To coin an expression, I tip my hat to you, Gussie!

Chapter 8

MILTON CHESTER MEMORIES

MY COUSIN, **ALEX CHESTER**, **ALSO** interviewed his father, Milton, and mother, Florence, on February 24, 2002. Milton was Gussie's son and my father's first cousin. Milton and his family lived on Houston Street in Manhattan, then moved to the Williamsburg section of Brooklyn, eventually to Freeport in Nassau County on Long Island. Later in life, Milton and Florence, Milton's brother, Bernie (the Roxy Candy Store owner), and his wife, Irene, moved to Delray Beach, Florida. Milton and Florence bought their residence; Bernie and Irene rented.

Milton and Florence were strangers to me until Alex C. brought them back to life. Alex and his sister, Lois, treasure the interview with Milton and were happy to share it with me. I learned more about Milton, part of the generation after Gussie's, from this interview. I discovered where Milton grew up, went to school, and then how he joined the army, proudly serving his country. Of course, Milton also remembered Gussie's delicatessens.

Here is a portion of that interview.

A: What I'd like to do is talk with you a little bit about your life and what you remember growing up. You were born in 1922 on April 1st, and your parents were Alex and Gussie. I wonder what you can tell us about growing up. What stories do you have?

M: *Very few. My mother and father were in the delicatessen business on the east side of New York. We were living on Houston Street in New York City.*

A: I remember that. I remember. It seemed like all the children helped.

M: *At the age of six, I guess, we moved to Williamsburg, and we got a delicatessen store. We lived at 327 South 3rd Street. How's that?*

A: That's pretty good.

M: *I attended PS 37 in Brooklyn. It was an old building with sliding doors that partitioned off different sections for meetings and instruction. Then I went to PS 50 in Brooklyn. We called it an intermediate school or junior high school through ninth grade. I attended rapid advanced classes, which put me ahead of my age group by about two years. I graduated from Junior High School 50, then attended Seward Park High School in New York City, just across the bridge from where we lived in Brooklyn. It was a brand new school, as opposed to my old building in Brooklyn. It was a local high school. I graduated from Seward Park High School at the age* *of sixteen and from Brooklyn College with a B.A. in Political Science and Economics. I attended from 1938 to 1942, at which time the war was raging in Europe. While I was attending school, the draft was on; everybody over eighteen had to register. I volunteered for the U.S. Army toward the end of 1942, which actually ensured I wouldn't have to take the final exams—they were automatic.*

A: So if you agreed to go into the army, they would...

M: *No, I volunteered.*

A: But you were still able to graduate?

M: *Yeah! I still graduated, but I didn't attend any graduation or anything. I was sent to Camp Upton.*

A: Was that in California?

M: *No. Camp Upton was right out on Long Island, and I know it was bitterly cold. This was in the heart of winter on Long Island. I went into the service right after Christmas. It was bitterly cold, and we were pretty much exposed to the elements in these barracks buildings without any heat or anything. We had pot-bellied stoves. I spent several weeks at Camp Upton because I had a clerical job working in the office before I was assigned to a basic training company. I'm pretty much vague about shipping out and where we even went. Oh, we went to California. I recall now.*

A: That's what I thought! Santa Anita?

M: *Santa Anita Racetrack. We had eight men sleeping*

where a very good horse used to sleep. At this point, I was working in this cadre, training cadre, at the camp, giving basic training to recruits. I was appointed instructor for ammunition companies, explosives companies. Also, I was assigned to a company that established ammunition dumps along the West Coast. So I was moving around pretty much, on what they called detached service. I was not assigned to anything, while getting in about ten basic training classes. I had plenty of basic training! I was transferred to a combat engineer company, which went to Camp Chaffee, Arkansas. From Camp Chaffee, we transferred out of the combat engineering company to London, England, after a trip of about nineteen days crossing the ocean.

A: That would have been about what? '43? '44?

M: *'43. The reason for such a long trip was that the convoy had to move at the slowest speed of any of the boats in the convoy, and they also spent time maneuvering and changing course, going back and forth to avoid enemy submarines, U-boats. I spent several months in England doing war repair damage from bombing. I then shipped out to a replacement company. They were stationed in Belgium. After arriving there and before I was assigned to anything, an opportunity came to go to Officers Training School and become an officer. The enticing part of this thing is that they were sending you back to France for the training—anything to get away* *from the front. So we shipped back and spent another eight or ten weeks of basic training. We went through OCS class in about ten weeks. By this time, the war was nearing an end. I was shipped to a replacement company to be assigned to the regular company. Just when I got there, peace had been declared, so that worked out very well. I was sent over to Germany to join the 3rd Division, 3rd Infantry Division, 15th Regiment.*

A: By this time you were a Second Lieutenant?

M: *By this time I was a Second Lieutenant assigned to the company, regimental company, 15th Regiment. After a few months, I was assigned to become an instructor at the local military school designed to give some training to the soldiers who wanted it — English language, German language and mathematics. It was the military's idea to stimulate and teach soldiers who were working independently. I was assigned to teach explosives and ammunition, which I'd been trained in, and also the basics of the German language. This lasted about a year, by which time I was eligible for discharge, having served over a year in the Army of Occupation. So I returned to the United States. That would be 1945, no, 1946.*

A: What part of Germany were you in?

M: *Actually, at the school, we were not in any particular camp. We were in an evacuated salt mine that the Germans had used as a military base.*

A: Do you remember what part of Germany it was?

M: *I'm trying to remember the names now. We were in Hersfeld, which w... Actually, Baden Nauheim in Germany. And Fulda, F-U-L-D-A, which was a main city of German Catholicism. Do you remember the town that was destroyed? Cologne?*

F: Cologne? Kassel.

M: *Kassel also. Actually, just across the line the Russians were occupying. We'd meet with the Russians quite frequently. We got along pretty well.*

A: I remember you talking about some of that occupation thing there, especially scrounging around for parts for keeping vehicles running.

M: *Yeah! Unfortunately, it was tough to get resupplied. Trucks with bad tires... broken windows. It was very difficult, really, to get replacement parts. Meanwhile, fifty miles from where we were, they'd established a depot to store all those army vehicles in preparation to be shipped to Japan. I discovered that this was so close to us. We'd get a truck, ask for volunteers, and we'd go out scrounging, and that means anything that we could possibly use. Throw the stuff in the truck and bring it back. We'd go with five or six volunteers in the truck and pull into the supply depot. I told the driver to keep going. I'll salute them, and you keep going. We'd drive in and park our truck alongside hundreds of other vehicles in the open. We'd go from one to the other, taking* *what we needed: tires, windshields. That's how we got a lot of equipment. It was illegal as hell, but we got it!*

A: Let's talk a little about, if you can remember, growing up in Williamsburg and working at the delicatessen: the things you did there, and things you were interested in... sports...

M: *I really don't remember too much when I was young. I know that we all pitched in at the store when we were there, whatever needed doing.*

A: So, did you work in the store after school and on weekends?

M: *We spent most of our time in the store because that's where we were living.*

F: Would you call it a happy time?

M: *Yeah, it was a very happy time. We had an apartment that we slept in. The rest of the day, we all spent at the store here, whether washing dishes, peeling potatoes, making potato salad or chopped liver. Laughter. Eating. We all pitched in because everybody had to work in order to make a living. As far as the store itself, as I say, we all cleaned tables, we delivered orders, whatever had to be done. We all worked behind the counter. We ate! (Laughter from everyone).*

F: Good stuff. They had good corned beef there. How much was a corned beef sandwich in those days?

M: *A corned beef sandwich was fifteen cents. Salami*

and bologna were ten cents.

F: French fries?

M: *Tongue was expensive, cost more than the corned beef.*

F: *I think French fries were a nickel or a dime. French fries were expensive.*

M: *Dime.*

F: Cole slaw and potato salad. A hot dog on a bun and sauerkraut?

M: *Five cents.*

A: Grandma talks about having several stores, several delicatessens. Was there just one that you remember?

M: *Only one that I remember. They had one when I was born on Houston Street. They had a store in East New York... Canarsie. New Lots Avenue. Then they opened a store on Bedford Avenue in Brooklyn, which is the one I remember.*

A: When did they sell that?

M: *Actually, they built the new store because there was a fire in the old one.*

F: And they had the store when Dorothy was married? She was married in '31?

M: *I believe so.*

F: And they moved shortly after that? 1940?

M: *Who moved?*

F: Your parents moved up to Monticello.

A: *So they sold the store and then basically retired to Monticello around 1940.*

M: *My father was sick. He really couldn't work. My mother ran the store.*

F: **Did they move there before you went into the service or after? Did they move to Monticello before you went into the service?**

M: *Yes.*

A: **Dad, it wasn't very usual for people to go to college back at that time in the '40s. Why did you decide to go, and was it expensive?**

M: *I was too young to work. (Laughter).*

A: **You'd already done your working.**

F: *He'd gotten out of school at sixteen.*

M: *Sixteen.*

A: **So you went to college at seventeen years old or so.**

M: *Sixteen. I was twenty when I graduated.*

A: **So I guess...was it very expensive to go?**

M: *Not in those days.*

F: **What college did you go to?**

M: *Brooklyn College. A city college. Minimum expense.*

F: **Where did you live at the time?**

M: *I lived with Dorothy.*

F: **What about Bernie?**

M: *Bernie went to high school in Jamaica.*

F: **Where did he live?**

M: *Flushing. He lived with Dorothy, too.*

F: **Oh, really? (Laughter). Uh-huh. You were running a boarding house?**

M: *Yeah.*

A: And that's because your parents moved to Monticello.

M: *Right.*

A: When they built the house up there, did they already have the bungalow colony as part of that property? Or was that added later?

M: *No. That was built after the house. The land wasn't doing anything. They had to bring in income, so they had the bungalow colony. I used to spend time with... my father was sick at the time and couldn't go to work. He used to keep them busy with these projects. So he spent time... he knew nothing about building, and neither did I, but we'd check out plans and books of plans. We'd pick out pictures that we liked and tried to incorporate them.*

A: What was your father's illness?

M: *I don't really know... whether he had a stroke... he had ulcers, bleeding ulcers.*

F: *Ulcers. I think it was bleeding ulcers.*

A: He was born in Lithuania.

F: *I think Ukraine.*

M: *I just really discovered not too long ago that Litvoks were from Lithuania.*

F: *No, it wasn't that simple.*

M: *But it was. Ukraine was a section of Russia.*

A: I should say that it is February 24, 2002. This will close the interview with Milton R. Chester, and after this interview, we still don't know what the "R" stands for.

F: *Oh, no! (Laughter).*

M: *Who knows? If I hadn't changed my name, you may not be in your position!*

A: (Chuckling). That's true. The names were so impermanent when they came to the United States. They were Melnitsa and there were Ukrainetz. Then they were Cohens, and there were Mandels, but they were all changed when they came to America, so you grew up as Cohen. What was Grandma's maiden name? She was a Melnitsa? Mandel?

M: *Mandel. We found out later. She came here; she was Gussie Mandel, but we found out they came over here as Melnitsa.*

A: Okay. Alright. Time to eat.

From what I learned, Milton and Florence Chester were loving, caring people. Their children, Alex and Lois, said that Milton and Florence were phenomenal parents who very much wanted to keep their family together. Milton and Florence had two other children, Mark, an attorney, and Eric, whom I met on a family Zoom meeting.

Family Zoom meetings are an important and most enjoyable way of connecting with my family. There are family members whom I have met only through such meetings. With so many people in different locations across the country and in Italy, these "computer connections" enable the family to stay in touch. Finding a time slot for these meetings to fit in with everyone's schedule can be challenging, but we do it. I look forward to more such meetings so we can all learn more about our "new" cousins.

To say the least, I wish that Milton and Florence had been a part of my life. I am grateful through genealogical research that I found them and their children. Alex and Lois's stories about their parents helped Milton and Florence become a part of my present-day family, where they will always have a place in my heart. My family tree is richer for having them as special branches. I will always have questions as to why my father never told us about this part of his family. The Chester family has been reunited with mine.

Milton Chester passed away on December 19, 2005, at age eighty-three in Delray Beach, Florida. His wife, Florence, died on February 6, 2014, at age eighty-eight. Both Milton and Florence are interred in Eternal Light Memorial Gardens in Boynton Beach, Florida.

PHOTOS AND DOCUMENTS

MADLYN EPSTEIN STEINHART

*My father, Manny Epstein, a military policeman
in Japan during WWII*

Family photo from my parents' wedding

Aunt Gussie and Great-Grandma Yetta at my parents' wedding

Cousins reunion luncheon at Ben's Deli in Boca Raton 2020

Rona and Maddy

Alex and Sherry Chester

JOSEF SPRINGER

Database of the Terezín inmates and persons deported to the Łódź and Minsk ghettoes and to the Ujazdów labor camp

First Name	Josef
Last Name (Maiden Name)	Springer
Birthdate	25. 4. 1898
Degree	MUDr.
Designation of Transport to Ujazdów (1942) and to the Ghettos Łódź (1941), Minsk (1941) and Terezín (1941-1945)	U, 28. 1. 1942, Brno → Terezín, 1000 ?
Transport Number to Ujazdów (1942) and to the Ghettos Łódź (1941), Minsk (1941) and Terezín (1941-1945)	909
Transport Number from the Ghetto Terezín (1941-1945)	Es, 19. 10. 1944, Terezín → Auschwitz, 1500
Designation of Transport from the Ghetto Terezín (1941-1945)	415
Fate	Died

Record of Josef Springer transported to Nazi Death Camp
(From Auschwitz Museum)

Transport paper of Josef Springer to Terezin
(From Auschwitz Museum)

BEILE SPRINGER

Beile Springer nee Melnitzer was born in Stobychwa, Poland in 1894 to Menakhem and Yenta. She was married to Yosef. Prior to WWII she lived in Kowel, Poland. During the war she was in Wolyn, Poland.

Beile was murdered in the Shoah (according to this source).

This information is based on a Page of Testimony (displayed here) submitted by her brother, Paul Mandel

⚑ During the Shoah, Jews were murdered in a variety of ways, among them gassing, shooting, burning, drowning or burial alive, exhaustion through forced labor, starvation, epidemic diseases, deprivation of medical care and minimal hygienic conditions, and more. Some Jews took their own lives in order to escape arrest and further persecution, or to end their hopeless, relentless suffering.

Last Name	Springer
Last Name	Shpringer
Last Name	Shpringer
First Name	Beile
First Name	Beila
First Name	Beile
Maiden Name	Melnitzer
Gender	Female
Date of Birth	1894
Place of Birth	Stobychwa,Kamien Koszyrski,Polesie,Poland
Father's First Name	Menakhem

Record of Bella Springer's death (From Yad Vashem)

<table>
<tr><td colspan="2">1, 1:59 PM   Central DB of Shoah Victims' Names - Record Details</td></tr>
<tr><td>Mother's First Name</td><td>Yente</td></tr>
<tr><td>Mother's First Name</td><td>Yenta</td></tr>
<tr><td>Marital Status</td><td>Married</td></tr>
<tr><td>Spouse's First Name</td><td>Yosef</td></tr>
<tr><td>Permanent Place of Residence</td><td>Kowel,Kowel,Wolyn,Poland</td></tr>
<tr><td>Place during the War</td><td>Wolyn,Poland</td></tr>
<tr><td>Place of Death</td><td>Wolyn,Poland</td></tr>
<tr><td>Status according to Source</td><td>murdered</td></tr>
<tr><td>Submitter's Last Name</td><td>Mandel</td></tr>
<tr><td>Submitter's First Name</td><td>Paul</td></tr>
<tr><td>Relationship to Victim</td><td>Brother</td></tr>
<tr><td>Source</td><td>Yad Vashem - Pages of Testimony Names Memorial Collection</td></tr>
<tr><td>Type of material</td><td>Page of Testimony</td></tr>
<tr><td>Item ID</td><td>1939715</td></tr>
<tr><td colspan="2">* Automatic translation from Hebrew</td></tr>
<tr><td colspan="2">⚠ The Names Database is a work in progress. Feedback, corrections and additions are welcome.</td></tr>
</table>

Paul Mandel's Testimony to Yad Vashem about his sister,
Bella Springer

YETTA MANKEL

YETTA MANKEL passed away on Thursday, June 2, 1955 and is located in block 9 of Montefiore Cemetery.

Interment #:	82036
Last Name:	MANKEL
First Name:	YETTA
Age:	82
Date of Death:	6/2/1955
Gate:	302/E
Block:	9
Row:	011L
Grave:	5
Section:	
Plot:	
Society Name:	CHEV. ATHERETH ZKEINIM

PHOTO REQUEST   PLANTINGS   SEASONAL CARE

STONE CLEANING

Record of Great-Grandma Yetta's burial site at Montefiore
Cemetery (Wrong spelling of name that led
to all the confusion)

From:
fran@montefiores.co
To: osa258@aol.com

Fri, Sep 19 at 2:02 PM

So far what I have found is that on the maps the last name is spelled as Mandel date of death 6/2/55 date of burial 6/3/55
And it shows that she does have a headstone.
So if you choose you can go on our website www.montefiores.org and purchase a photo of the stone for $16.00
Her interment # is 82036.

I will still try to find the time to locate any original paperwork, but you may get the photo faster.

Sincerely,
Francine
Montefiore Cemetery
718-528-1700 x 100

Email from Montefiore Cemetery identifying Yetta Mandel

Grandma Bertha and my sister, Meryl

Location of one of Gussie's delicatessens

The Roxy in Monticello, NY

Rona's mother Sydell

Bertha Epstein's burial record

Milton Epstein's burial record

Bernard Chester

BERNARD CHESTER
DELRAY BEACH, FL AND MONTICELLO, NY

Bernard Chester a retired business owner and longtime area resident died on Wednesday, January 2, 2008 in Hospice by the Sea Boca Raton, Fl. He was 82.

Bernie was born in Brooklyn, NY on April 4, 1925 the son of Alex and Gussie Mandel Chester. He was World War II Army Veteran. He was a member of the JWV, the Knights of Phthisis and Workman Circle Brand #610 Monticello

He is survived by his wife Irene at home, his two sons; Jeffrey Chester and his wife Kathleen on Monticello and Stewart Chester and his wife Patrice of Rock Hill, his sister; Dorothy Mar of Florida and his three grandchildren; Jamie Chester of NYC, Lyndsey Lentini of Kiamesha and Devon Chester of Rock Hill and his great granddaughter Alessia Lentini.

Funeral services will be held on Sunday, January 6, 2008 at 1pm in the Joseph N. Garlick Funeral Home Inc 388 Broadway Monticello, NY. Burial will be in the Workman Circle #610 Cemetery Thompson Rd Monticello.

Funeral arrangements by Joseph N. Garlick Funeral Home Inc. Monticello. For directions or to send the family a condolence note visit our website at www.josephngarlickfuneralhome.com.

Bernard Chester's obituary

Irene Mildred Chester

Irene Chester, retired clerk with the New York State Dept. of Labor and long time resident of Monticello and Delray beach, Fl, died unexpectedly Saturday, May 28, 2011 at Boca Community Hospital, Boca Raton, FL. She was 84.

The daughter of the late David and Gussie Wolf (nee Blatt), Irene was born on December 8, 1926.

She is survived by her two sons; Jeffrey Chester and his wife, Kathleen, ofKiamesha Lake and Stewart Chester and his wife, Patrice of Rock Hill; her brother, Abe Wolf of Sun City, Arizona; her sister, Ann Milofsky of Sun City, Arizona; her three grandchildren: Jamie Chester of NYC, Lyndsey Lentini of Bethel and Devon Chester of Rock Hill; her two great grandchildren, Alessia Emanuela Lentini and Niccolo Bernardo Lentini of Bethel, as well as many nieces and nephews.

Irene was predeceased by her husband, Bernard.

Funeral services will be held on Wednesday, June 1, 2011 at 11:00am at Joseph N. Garlick Funeral Home, 388 Broadway, Monticello, NY. Burial will follow in the Workman's Circle #610 Cemetery, Thompson Road, Monticello.

Memorial contributions may be made to the Cystic Fibrosis Foundation of Greater NY, 2975 Westchester Ave., Suite 204, Purchase, NY 10577. (www.cysticfibrosis.com)

Funeral arrangements are by Joseph N. Garlick Funeral Home, Monticello, NY. For directions or further information please visit www.josephngarlickfuneralhome.com or call 845-794-7474.

Irene Chester's obituary

Neighborhood Directory Bronx 1960
(Fieldson, Riverdale, Spuyten Duyvil)

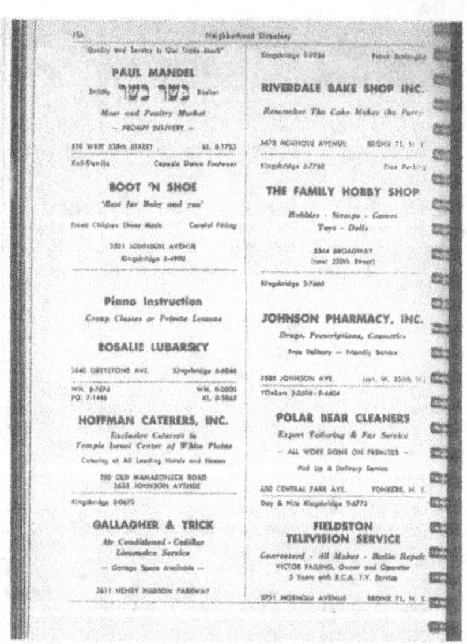

Advertisement of Paul Mandel's Meat and Poultry Market
(From Neighborhood Directory)

INSURANCE

DANTE S. CAPUTO	101 W. 31st Street	LO 4-2770	32
	5288 Sycamore Avenue 71	KI 9-7308	
PHILIP L. CASAZZA	8767 Liebig Avenue 71	KI 9-8036	120
DAVID L. GLASS	545 W. 236th Street 63	KI 8-4019	142
SAMUEL D. ROSAN AGENCY INC.	14 Maiden Lane	BE 3-8114	68

INTERIOR DECORATORS

FAY & SON	6543 Broadway 71	KI 9-7643	82
MARTIN KUCKLY	200 East 72nd Street	YU 8-3008	126
WILLIAM L. KUNZE	3706 Riverdale Avenue 63	KI 3-3011	56
KARL SCHMID	541 So. Broadway, Yonkers	YO 3-2383	139
WALD DECORATORS	306 W. 231st Street 63	LO 2-8677	144

JEWELRY & JEWELRY REPAIRING

BEERMAN JEWELERS	427 So. Broadway, Yonkers	YO 3-2641	190
EDWIN P. HENSCHEL	70 Montgomery Circle, New Rochelle	NE 2-9686	130
THE JEWEL SHOP	3261 Johnson Avenue 63		132
JOVE'S JEWELRY	5561 Broadway 63	KI 3-6717	148
KURTZ JEWELERS	466 So. Broadway, Yonkers	YO 8-4831	168
NIESLER'S	213 W. 231st Street 63	KI 3-2287	146
RELIABLE JEWELERS	213 W. 231st Street 63	KI 3-2287	146
WATCH & CLOCK SHOP	508 So. Broadway, Yonkers	YO 8-7765	90
WAYNE SILVERSMITHS INC.	546 So. Broadway, Yonkers	YO 3-6962	138

KOSHER MEATS

AL BERTENTHAL	215 W. 231st Street 63	KI 3-0603	162
MORRIS BRETTSCHNEIDER	235 W. 231st Street 63	KI 8-0866	138
PAUL MANDEL	570 W. 235th Street 63	KI 8-1723	156
RELIABLE KOSHER MEATS	3536 Johnson Avenue 63	KI 6-2224	158

LAMP REPAIRS

MACFABEL ANTIQUES	374 Riverdale Ave., Yonkers	YO 3-7293	130

LANDSCAPE GARDENER

BROADWAY NURSERY	6731 Broadway 63	KI 3-0912	76
D. CORASANITI	38 Westerly St., Yonkers	YO 5-7920	134
T. H. FELLHEIMER	3610 Tibbett Avenue 63	KI 6-2566	120

LAUNDRIES

CAMBRIDGE HAND LAUNDRY	503 W. 236th Street 63	KI 3-3433	162
COLGATE AUTOMATIC LAUNDRY	164 W. 231st Street 63	KI 6-3632	142
SILVER LINING LAUNDRY	157 Riverdale Ave., Yonkers	YO 3-7300	2
		KI 9-7745	
VAN CORTLANDT HAND LAUNDRY	436 W. 238th Street 63	KI 8-0822	130

Listing of Paul Mandel's Meat and Poultry Market
(Address and phone number from Neighborhood Directory)

2220459

Please inscribe the name of each victim of the Holocaust on a separate form.
Additional forms can be obtained from the

YAD VASHEM
Martyrs' and Heroes'
Remembrance
Authority

די־י־ד
עדות־בלאט

A Page of Testimony

THE MARTYRS' AND
HEROES' REMEMBRANCE
LAW, 5713—1953
determines in article No. 2
that —
The task of YAD VASHEM
is to gather into the homeland
material regarding all those
members of the Jewish people
who laid down their lives, who
fought and rebelled against the
Nazi enemy and his collabora-
tors, and to perpetuate their
memory and that of the
communities, organizations, and
institutions which were destroyed because they were Jewish.

1953 ... תשי"ג

Photo

1. Family name — (SPRINGER, BEILE)

2. First Name (maiden name)

3. Date of birth — 1894, around Dec

4. Place of birth

5. Name of father

6. Name of mother

7. Name of spouse
(if a wife, add maiden name)

8. Place of residence before the war

9. Places of residence during the war

10. Circumstances of death (place, date, etc.)

I, the undersigned
residing at (full address) — Paul Mandel 251 NE 187 St Miami 33179

relationship to deceased

hereby declare that this testimony is correct to the best of my knowledge.

Place and date — Signature — Paul Mandel

— even unto them will I give in mine house and within my
walls a place and a name...that shall not be cut off. —

Return to: Community Relations Committee
Greater Miami Jewish Federation
4200 Biscayne Boulevard
Miami, FL 33137
Phone: (305) 576-4000

(Call us for information and
additional copies)

Paul Mandel's Testimony to Yad Vashem (Hebrew)

Mother's First Name	Yente
Mother's First Name	Yenta
Marital Status	Married
Spouse's First Name	Yosef
Permanent Place of Residence	Kowel,Kowel,Wolyn,Poland
Place during the War	Wolyn,Poland
Place of Death	Wolyn,Poland
Status according to Source	murdered
Submitter's Last Name	Mandel
Submitter's First Name	Paul
Relationship to Victim	Brother
Source	Yad Vashem - Pages of Testimony Names Memorial Collection
Type of material	Page of Testimony
Item ID	1939715

* Automatic translation from Hebrew

⚠ The Names Database is a work in progress. Feedback, corrections and additions are welcome.

Paul Mandel's Testimony to Yad Vashem
(Translated to English)

GUSSIE COHEN

GUSSIE COHEN passed away on Saturday, May 10, 1980 and is located in section 3, block 36 of Beth Moses Cemetery.

Interment #:	B26837
Last Name:	COHEN
First Name:	GUSSIE
Age:	71
Date of Death:	5/10/1980
Cemetery:	Beth Moses Cemetery
Section:	3
Block:	36 View Block Map*
Row:	11
Grave:	24
Divsion:	C
Plot:	SO.AVE-BIALIK RD
Society Name:	ADATH ISRAEL OF BROOKLYN BLOCK 36
Stone Type:	Headstone

* Organization names are subject to change.

Gussie Cohen's burial record

Milton Chester Obituary

Chester, Milton R., 83 of Delray Beach, FL passed away on December 19, 2005. Riverside Gordon Memorial Chapel, Delray Beach.

To plant trees in memory, please visit the Sympathy Store.

Published by Sun-Sentinel on Dec. 24, 2005.

Milton Chester Obituary (South Florida Sun Sentinel)

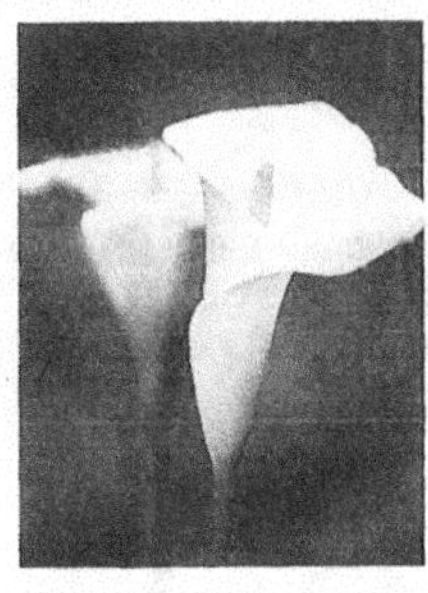

Florence Chester
OBITUARY

Florence Chester, age 88, of Delray Beach died on Feb. 6th. Beloved wife of the late Milton Chester. Devoted Mother of Alex, Lois, Mark and Eric Chester. Dear Sister of Ruth Asser and Harvey Guzik. Loving Sister-In-Law of Dorothy Margulies. Cherished Grandmother of Grayson, Seaver and Megan. Services at Riverside Gordon Memorial Chapels, 7205 W. Atlantic Ave., Delray Beach, FL on Sunday, Feb. 9th at 2PM. Expressions of Sympathy in her memory may be donated to the charity of your choice. Memorial Observance will be held Sunday-Tuesday from 6-9PM.

Share this obituary:

Birth: May 2, 1925
Death: February 6, 2014

Published in the Sun Sentinel from February 8, 2014 to February 10, 2014.

Florence Chester Obituary (South Florida Sun Sentinel)

Dorothy and Alexa

Alan R. and his dog Solo

Rona's dog Mylie

Alexa's dog Marshmallow

Alan R. as a boy with his dog

Cousins lunch in Boca Raton March 2026
Top Row L-R Lois, Rona, Tracy (Rona's daughter), Maddy
Bottom Row L-R Dona, Rick, Howie

Chapter 9

Dogs Are Family Too

WHILE TALKING WITH MY NEWLY discovered cousins about our families, I found that they greatly loved animals... especially dogs. Many cousins had dogs as pets. Could this be part of our family's DNA? Are we all inclined to love four-legged furry creatures? My dad had a dog named Smitty, but I didn't know much about him. Did my dad's love of dogs pass down to me? Yes! Is there a biological reason for this? Quite possibly.

According to an article by Mindi Weisberger published in the May 22, 2019, edition of *Live Science*, there may very well be an explanation. Scientists have recently discovered that people who love dogs may do so partly because of their DNA. Researchers suggested people who show the greatest love for animals may exhibit personality traits such as empathy, compassion, and a preference for nonconformity. These are the words of the scientists, not mine. These traits might have a genetic component.

Scientists at the Roslin Institute and Scotland's Rural

College conducted a study where the DNA of one hundred and sixty-one student volunteers was analyzed. The volunteers also answered a series of questions. The scientists discovered that those in the study who showed the most compassion for animals had a version of a gene called oxytocin, called the "love hormone" by scientists. According to the study, women were more positive than men. Quoting Dr. Sarah Brown of the Roslin Institute, "We already knew that oxytocin was important for empathy between people, but now we know it helps us bond with animals too."

Another study, from the University of Liverpool, claimed that being a dog lover is in one's genes and DNA. Oxytocin was evident in those monitored in the study. According to Professor Carri Westgarth, "Genetics and environment play equal roles in determining dog ownership." Now that we know there is increased oxytocin in dog owners, scientists believe there is a genetic attachment to loving dogs.

You know that warm feeling you get when cuddling your favorite blanket? That's how I feel when I hug a dog. Sorry, cat lovers... I don't feel the same way about cats. I love to look at their whiskers, but my feline friends don't give me the fuzzy feeling that a dog does. Man's best friend is this woman's best friend, too. When I was two years old, visiting family in the Catskills, I met a collie in the hotel that followed me everywhere. That's probably how my love for dogs started. There are three cartoon dogs that I have been madly in love with. Astro from *The Jetsons* and Dino from *The Flintstones* are both Hanna-Barbera characters who show lots of love to everyone. Charlie Brown's dog, Snoopy, is the rock star of all cartoons. He is the greatest of all time!

What about dogs makes so many people fall in love with them? Is it a dog's face that makes humans smile? Is it a wagging tail? Why do we melt when it appears as if dogs smile back at us? Are they mimicking our behavior? Yes, dogs have an innate ability to react. They smile and interact very positively when it is unexpected. According to Pawtique.com, a website for a dog photography company based in England, dogs' natural behaviors result in "posing" when they feel comfortable in familiar surroundings.

They don't pose like humans, but their behaviors make it seem that way. They don't need to be trained to pose. How often have you seen photos and videos of a dog playing in water? It's an action dogs love to do, and people love watching dogs frolicking. It's another one of the behaviors we adore. All of these questions and traits lead to one very unscientific answer: Simply put, our family loves dogs! Yes... there's a dog for almost every household. The love of animals seems prevalent throughout my family, with many relatives having dogs as part of their homes.

When my dad died, my sister and I wanted a dog. Our mother told us to ask our grandmother, Bertha. Grandma said no, so my sister and I never got that dog, probably because of the cost. If my husband weren't so highly allergic to dogs, we would have had a collie, a beagle, a husky, or a German shepherd.

I love caring for my neighbor's dog, Charlie, a Yorkie.

He always runs to me, greeting me with loving licks, never judging me. When our neighbors go away for the day or overnight, we help out with Charlie. He's so adorable when slurping up his dinner from his bowl. With many restaurants allowing dogs into their premises, some establishments now offer "Puppy Cups," a small-sized portion of food to feed Spot or Rover. Some Starbucks stores have recently adopted this policy.

My sister, Meryl, and brother-in-law, Tony, had a Doberman, Dillon, who, if he knew you, would greet you with love and slobbering kisses. If Dillon didn't know or recognize you, he would snarl at you while exposing his large teeth in a threatening way. Fortunately, Dillon liked me. Others weren't so lucky.

My Oklahoma cousin, Alex Resnick, is known to his family as the "Animal Whisperer" because he and his family help rescue dogs, reunite lost dogs with their human families, and foster dogs until they come to stay with their new forever families. Anyone who takes on the task of fostering animals should be admired. Sharing their home with a needy animal demonstrates more than sympathy and empathy. It is love to the highest level.

Alex had a dog named Aurora, part husky and part wolf, who was the smallest of the litter. Aurora originally belonged to Alex's son, Phillip, who attended the University of Oklahoma. When Phillip moved to a place where he could not have a dog, Aurora moved in with Alex, where she became his service dog until she became ill and passed away. The family was devastated. Alex's son and daughter-in-law have two other dogs nowadays, Tovah and Bowie, both part huskies. Alex's mother, Minnie, had two dogs, a collie named Marin and a poodle named JoJo.

Alex Resnick's daughter, Anna Henson, and her husband, Dusty, live in southeast Oklahoma with their family of dogs, Daisy, Harper, and Wallace. In the summer of 2024, an injured Great Pyrenees was spotted near the river cabin that Anna and Dusty own. They called the dog Lady. A neighbor was able to coax Lady to the property that they share with Anna and Dusty. Gradually, Lady trusted the neighbors enough to allow them to get close, and they gave her a bed and fed her. Over time, after the neighbors moved away, Lady became closer to Anna and Dusty and stayed on their property. Eventually, Lady let Anna and Dusty feed and love her; however, Lady growled at the other three dogs but wasn't aggressive. During a cold spell, Lady bonded more with Dusty.

During the months that followed, Lady disappeared in the forest. Dusty kept looking for Lady, eventually finding her. She was scared, frail, and starving. Lady remembered Dusty and allowed him to pick her up and put her in his car. Dusty then drove home to Oklahoma City with Lady, where she received proper medical care, nutrition, and love. Lady has recovered and now lives with Dusty, Anna, their daughter, and their three other dogs, playing outside, enjoying a life of love, luxury, and protecting the family.

Alex R.'s nephew, my cousin, Allen Rosenbloom, had an Australian Shepherd named Solo who crossed the

Rainbow Bridge. Solo was fondly remembered. Allen told me, "Solo was more than a companion, loved by the entire family. Solo was part of the family." Allen's previous dogs, Buffy, a pit bull, and Marvin, a collie, were incredibly sweet.

Cousin Alex Chester and his wife, Sherry, have a large menagerie in their home, providing lots of love. Alex grew up with animals: dogs, cats, birds, and many wild rehabbed animals. Nowadays, Alex and Sherry care for Opus, a white-fronted Amazon parrot, and Carra Burn, a Gordon Setter. Their Irish Setter/Golden Setter mix, Caylie, recently passed.

My cousin, Alexa, and her husband, Marv, owned two dogs: Marshmallow, a white German Shepherd who is no longer with us, and Rosie, a Golden Retriever—a real sweetie who always loves to play with Alexa.

Shortly after I met my cousin, Rona, I met and fell in love with her dogs, Mylie, a Shiba Inu, and Tori, a chow/shepherd mix. Mylie and Tori came to me immediately. They were delightful. I couldn't get over the love and acceptance. I never had a dog and felt as if they were mine. With every visit to their house, those dogs gave me a love I hadn't felt in a long time. I was crushed when Rona told me Tori recently crossed the Rainbow Bridge. Rona told me that her first dog, Punky, was a Lhasa Apso/Terrier mix that she got from a neighbor when their dog had a litter. Punky looked like a miniature sheepdog who grew to twenty-five pounds, living to age seventeen and a half. Rona also owned Samantha, a Shiba Inu/Lab mix, a breed she wanted after doing extensive research.

I like to think that Solo, Tori, Punky, Samantha, and Marshmallow are playing with chewy toys in a wide-open field.

Skippy, a Golden Retriever, was owned by my sister-in-law and her kids. He might have been the most gorgeous, loving dog I've ever known. Whenever he saw me, he remembered the belly rubs and back scratches I gave him when he was a puppy. He would come up to me without any prompting and put his paw on my hand, telling me he wanted me to pet or rub him, or to certainly not stop petting or rubbing him. We had a special bond. When Skippy needed medical treatment, I took care of him while he was wearing his special t-shirt and collar. Skippy has become the dog greeter at the Rainbow Bridge when dogs pass away. I still cry to this day when I think about him.

Dog charities have always been important to me. I support Best Friends, Broadway Barks, and the ASPCA. I hope to do more volunteer work with them, raising money for the charities via my daily exercise walks.

I love to be hands-on with dogs. I never met one that didn't love a belly rub, back scratch, or big hug. When a dog responds to you, the love lasts forever.

Chapter 10

WHERE DO WE GO FROM HERE?

ONE OF THE REASONS FOR writing this book was to inform younger and future generations about their ancestors and great-grandparents' families. Not only were there questions to be answered about nameless people in photographs, or names mentioned at family gatherings, but I wanted to give a sense of lineage, relatives, kinship, circle, and group dynamics that compose who they are and where they come from. Children have a right to know!

The history of someone's family makes them more complete and answers many, but not all, questions of why and who they are. All people should know their families. I hope everyone will know their families and not have to wait to find and seek them out. On my father's side of the family tree, hazel eyes, auburn or brown hair, and a love of all animals have been displayed for generations. One must know about their entire family to feel whole, appreciate, and understand who they are.

My father lived only to the age of forty-five and

missed many significant parts and major events of our lives. He never got to know the family I have discovered, appreciated, and loved. Newly discovered relatives want to know about my dad, and I have gladly shared many stories with them. I had to break down the walls my father forced us to live behind—not just to find out why he did what he did, but for me to grow as a person. The parent whom I loved the most is the parent who disappointed me the most. I have laughed and cried from memories, more crying than laughing. Both emotions have helped me grow.

Five years ago, I undertook a project to get as complete, or almost as complete, a picture of my family and who we are. Who are "our" people? Where would this continuously unfolding journey take me? When I started this assignment, I didn't want to be intolerant or prejudiced against anyone or anything I found. I had to keep an open mind, no matter what or who I discovered. I think I have done that.

Will future generations know and care about who came before us? Once I traced my genealogy going back a century and more, I wanted to go in the opposite direction and share this information with the younger generation. I have planted seeds. Now let the stories bloom. I am sharing everything I've learned with the younger generation and hope they will do the same decades down the road. Is it left to me to be the family storyteller? I can only dream that I have enabled others to take over. Perhaps this work will be part of my legacy.

My older nieces and nephews have been given

volumes of information about their ancestors and heritage; however, there are cousins out there who don't know, don't want to know, or are unaware of the existence of other members of their own family. You are who you are based on all members of your family. Things passed down to us make us who we are. None of us can plan this. We are the products of our past, living in the present, bringing our ancestors and their history into the future.

Decisions made and actions taken by our ancestors decades and centuries ago have led to who and where we all are today. Learn about, honor, and appreciate the people you never knew—those who came before. Without them, you would not be here. Make them proud. Share accomplishments. Finding your family will develop a strong spirit of community. I continue to think about the word "legacy." There is no financial or property bequest here. I have received the gift of family and discovering ancestors, people who, until this research, I never knew existed.

The only guarantee in genealogical research is that people are out there. It's up to you to use the right tools to find them. Entries on Ancestry.com can be wrong. Don't be disheartened. There is hope out there.

Once you decide to start looking for your ancestors, introducing yourself to your local librarian or computer coordinator can help in your search. They can help with access to websites that you've never heard of and assist in finding periodicals and documents. The challenge you face seeking previously unknown ancestors looks you in the eye as if daring you to proceed.

A daunting challenge, but the resulting jubilation when you are successful makes your efforts incredibly worthwhile. Be determined to succeed. You cannot let yourself fail. Staying positive when your research world is not on an even keel is crucial to keeping your focus. Remain determined in your search. These words may sound like clichés. They are not. They are words of advice or wisdom to encourage you in your search.

New adventures awaited me with every uncovered document. What was the historical context? How was this discovery connected to me and my family? What path would and should I take to reach the next find? Where and how could I figure out my and my family's place in history?

All of this new information makes me more complete. I am a product of people I never knew. I have a greater sense of family. In finding my family, my sense of self changed. I never had the full picture of who I was or where I came from. Now I have a better idea. I was an outsider meeting a disparate group of people—people whose lives were so different from mine.

Each of my discoveries has been treated with a quiet dignity, reverence, and respect, while, at the same time, a feeling of joy accompanied by the loud sound of a baseball player's walkup music. Each of these discovered descendants made the right decisions that led to what they became and to all of us being here today. I didn't want my ancestors to be forgotten. Somehow, after all their tragedies, suffering, and sacrifices, they had to live on. My ancestors were part of our nation of immigrants at a time when all were welcome. Nowadays, there's no guarantee that the same holds.

Through the marvel and beauty of modern technology, an eight-year-old girl from Oklahoma City, Oklahoma, can't wait to learn more about her newly discovered five-year-old cousin in Staten Island, New York, who loves American Girl dolls. Some family members follow the baseball achievements of a teenage pitcher from Parkland, Florida, who collects baseball cards with his grandfather. A musician from California strikes a chord and is sharing his new work across the country. A six-year-old boy, fascinated by trains, dinosaurs, and bugs, amazes his family with his intelligence. Another cousin loves to care for iguanas. A bicycle race rider from Tavares, Florida, shares his travel experiences of racing at locations nowhere near his home.

Our clan has grown to include teachers, lawyers, writers, a corporate event planner, a college professor, a nurse, a business executive, an assistant principal, a social worker turned medical librarian, an electrical engineer, a business management specialist, a martial arts instructor, and a pair of science researchers. In our ever-changing world, it is my great hope that our family can contribute and serve positively. Civic responsibility ranks very high in my playbook. Become an advocate for your family and colleagues.

Don't be afraid of the internet and the places you will search, but be careful. Yes, there are bad guys out there who look to hurt and steal from anyone. While many exits along the internet highway will take you off your course, you must persevere in your task. You cannot be defeated early. Keep pushing for answers. If you can't find them, talk to family, friends, neighbors, and friends of neighbors. You might be surprised by the information they might have or remember.

Look for chat rooms on social media sites. Once, while researching my husband's paternal family, I came across the daughter of an ex-wife of my husband's biological grandfather. The daughter had Social Security documents and Naturalization papers that the family had never seen before. If you're going to look for your family, you have to commit to the time needed to research. You have to do it right. A half-hearted effort may bear some fruit, but why be satisfied with dessert when a gourmet meal awaits? At the end of the day, the success you achieve will result from the hard work you do. Be your research army. Very few of us have the resources (money, time, ability to travel to find documents, hiring a team of professionals) to get the results we hope for.

Listen to the military stories when our veterans talk about World War II, Korea, Vietnam, and the Middle East. The memories and people won't be around forever. Honor them. Respect them. Thank them for their service while you hear the same story for the second, fifth, or tenth time. These brave men and women have families. Some might be yours or know about yours.

An old family tradition may become new when looked at by a fresh set of eyes. Don't be afraid of change, but at the same time, don't forget the past. Timeless traditions can be, and are, wonderful, but who's to say that your family celebrations can't be tweaked by adding a new twist? Maybe inviting friends and neighbors who don't celebrate your holidays can expand everyone's horizons... let alone share culture and stories. Food and drink go a long way when sharing. Try breaking bread together!

There are many documents and websites to help you in your search. You have to know where to look. If you want hard copies of documents, some are free; other records you must pay for. There is an untapped opportunity with research. Exhilarate in the research and discovery experience. The 1950 United States Census was released to the public on April 1, 2022, allowing researchers to access documents previously unseen by the public. The 1960 Census will be released to the public in April 2032. Just think of the juicy morsels one could add to their genealogical searches.

When searching for non-Jewish ancestors, one must search through church records. Documents of baptisms, confirmations, communions, marriages, and funerals may be obtained through a parish. You must know the exact church or parish to get a copy of the record. You may have to contact the local archdiocese to obtain specific information about which parish to contact or if a parish has closed.

As a retired teacher, I wanted to share my love of learning. Science, technology, and the internet enabled me to do just that. Something inside of me wanted to inspire others to explore the unknown, experience the highs and lows of discovery, and then report their findings. Once a teacher, always a teacher. My narrative is not the same as anyone else's. We all have routes to explore. Long-lost or hidden family secrets should re-emerge for everyone in the family to discuss and debate. Family genealogy is all-inclusive. If my journey has inspired anyone else, I have been successful.

In Chapter Two, I mentioned a genealogical jigsaw puzzle. The more I researched, the more pieces of the puzzle I found, until I hit the inevitable roadblock. There were some documents I could not find, but I won't stop looking.

Earlier in the book, I mentioned the word "closure." As my research went on, I realized that I would never have one hundred percent closure. There were and are too many unknowns, too many potholes to fill. To say the least, I can say I have done my best to tie up as many of the loose ends as possible, enabling my family and me to weave a new family narrative. At best, I have more family than I could ever have imagined.

There was and is a rich, vibrant tapestry about my family lineage, a history I enjoyed discovering. My family and I are innocent victims of something we never knew about from many years ago, and we still don't have the answers today. What happened in my family? Was it bad blood? Jealousy? Family feud? We'll never know. What can be said is that we are not allowing events that happened in our ancestors' past to negatively shape our family's future. Having said that, where do I and we go from here? My family and I are moving forward as a united family, all because of some genealogical research.

Epilogue

IT HAS BEEN OVER FIVE years since I started researching and writing about the maternal side of my father's family. Why did I look for them? What started as a purely accidental occurrence while working as a search angel helping someone search for their family turned into an effort that consumed me. It was purely a case of being in the right place at the right time to start searching for more of my roots. Online research and repeated emails brought me to a fascinating discovery: a cousin I never knew I had.

I have many questions for my parents and relatives that will forever go unanswered. Whatever reasons my parents and grandparents had for not staying in touch with certain members of the family are and were theirs, answers that I, and present-day family members, will never be able to figure out. None of my cousins has answers. I accept that, but we all wonder why.

My discoveries simply did not acknowledge that I and my immediate family existed. We are trying to make up for all of that as much as we can. To many of us, some of our fifty- or sixty-year-old memories feel like yesterday—family memories, albeit incomplete ones. Our legacy is that whatever happened in the past will not have any bearing on what will happen in the future. Grandchildren, great-grandchildren, great-nieces, and nephews will know our descendants and us. We have started the reconnection by sharing stories and pictures. Reunions are being planned.

In searching for my family, I have found myself, at age sixty-eight, still a work in progress. Too much time has been spent questioning the differences between selfishness and selflessness. It is not an easy task. It is a matter of getting negative thoughts, memories, and actions out of my mind, and changing my perspective. I have missed many opportunities out of doubt and fear. The words "doubt" and "fear" will no longer have a place in my heart and mind.

Writing, whether it be this story or my poetry, has been my therapy. The more I write, the better I feel. The shy little girl finally found the courage to spread her wings and fly. Meeting and starting to know my family later in life is a very precious gift.

When you place yourself second or third to others, something has to give and change. Finally, I've started that process. Some family members like that, others hate it. Lessons learned the hard way taught me that I am nothing to family or friends if I don't care about myself first.

I may never know more about my family. Technology

and resources, as helpful and great as they are, don't have all of the answers. No matter what information is at your disposal, there is more out there. Some of that information may never be found, but I will still search for it. Some documents are lost forever. There is nothing I or we can do to get them back.

When my Aunt Bella, Uncle Josef, and their children's deaths during the Holocaust were researched, the Jewish history in the family was resurrected. I knew my grandmother was raised Orthodox because she pre-arranged her funeral in Orthodox customs. She was buried in a plain wooden box, which we asked the funeral home to cover.

I was never exposed to that part of my religion. I have encountered the Orthodox Jewish community, but being a Reformed Jewish person is quite different, particularly when there are members of your family and close friends who practice other religions. Not only do I accept that, but it is a part of my life.

Life was difficult decades ago when my relatives came to New York. Looking to start a new life, they created and developed businesses and raised families. Losing family members during the Holocaust must have been horrible; the family grief lasts forever. These are facts my family and I never knew. I believe that siblings and their mother, my great-grandmother, knew, but I don't think my father and his cousins knew, because it was never discussed.

Not only am I happy that we have researched it, but we have the paperwork and facts about how Bella, Josef, and their children were lost. We have found them, but there is still much more to learn. I am still researching the Springer Family, but as I write this, we have not learned very much. Never one to give up, I check many resources from time to time about the Springer Family in the United States and Great Britain.

My new family has become my team... my special support squad. Their encouragement throughout this journey has taken me from an unknown family member to a new family leader... one who continues to develop and cultivate relationships, building towards a larger, closer kin.

Great-Grandma

My research stepped in, and so did long-lost relatives.

This is an homage to families everywhere.

How they are comprised doesn't matter.

They are family.

Many secrets, scars, and unopened doors are still there, but many people, whether they know it or not, may come across this and decide if it is important to delve into it.

Writing this is one thing, but making sense of it and accepting it is quite another.

Some people don't want to know, and some can't wait to start the journey.

Being the very best you can be might be a cliche, but being a work in progress involves polishing what is inside of you and listening to others, not just hearing them.

You can get people in without changing who you are.

You never know who benefits.

Great-Grandma Yetta, do you see what you created?
My hope is that you can acknowledge all of you are
loved too.

I never met Yetta, but I hope she knows her great-grandchildren found each other, along with the next generations, because of this book and others like it.

Madlyn Epstein Steinhart

ACKNOWLEDGEMENTS

THERE ARE SO MANY PEOPLE that I must thank who helped or encouraged me during my search for my family. Professor Henry Louis Gates, Jr., inspired me via his fantastic television program, *Finding Your Roots*. I will always be grateful. His associate, Cece Moore, taught me what DNA and science can lead to in searching. Both of you are amazing!

My cousin, Jake Garfinkle, provided lots of information about my ancestors and their homeland. My cousins, Rona, Dona, Alex C., Alex R., Lois, Stewart, Allen, and Larree shared wonderful stories about family I never knew. I am so thankful you are a part of my family now. To my editor/hubby, Howie, words cannot express how much I appreciate the job you have done. I can never forget the many long talks with my sister, Meryl, about our dad and family. I hope you're proud.

A very special thank you to my friends, Sori, Jeanette, Ellen, Zona, Leslee, Rita, and Vivian—your support throughout this process was incredibly uplifting. I send a tremendous thank you to Cheryl Benton and the Three Tomatoes Publishing Company for never-ending inspiration. I hope you like the story.

To all the professionals at the Dorot Jewish Division of the New York Public Library, New York City Search Center, The Center for Jewish History, The New York City Archives, Ancestry.com, The Catskill Borscht Belt Museum, The Catskills Institute, and The Arolsen Archives (part of the Auschwitz Museum), thank you for putting up with me and my many questions. Tremendous gratitude goes to Janet Munch, the Special Collections Librarian at Lehman College, for finding documents my family thought were lost forever. The picture of The Roxy in Monticello comes from the book "Images of America," published by Arcadia Press in 2010. Tom Rue gets credit for the photo.

I must mention and give special thanks to Francine Chiarotti from Montefiore Cemetery for unraveling the mystery of the whereabouts of my great-grandmother, Yetta—a mystery my family could never solve.

To all my fellow poets on HelloPoetry.com, and anyone who dares to create, keep on writing.

About the Author

MADLYN EPSTEIN STEINHART is a retired New York City teacher. She is a recipient of the prestigious Jessie McCanse Award from the National Telemedia Council and was chosen as a New York City Champion Teacher by C-SPAN. Maddy has published three books of poetry: *Beautiful Heart, Put Your Boots on and Dance in the Rain,* and *Shades of Grey.* She is also a researcher who helps adoptees find their birth families. *Found at Last* tells the story of finding her family.